Fostering Entrepreneurship in Georgia

DIRECTIONS IN DEVELOPMENT
Private Sector Development

Fostering Entrepreneurship in Georgia

Smita Kuriakose, Editor

THE WORLD BANK
Washington, D.C.

Contents

Tables

Acknowledgments

This book was authored and edited by Smita Kuriakose (economist, World Bank). Significant inputs were provided by Nana Adeishvili (consultant, World Bank), Murat Seker (economist, World Bank), Christina Tippmann (consultant, World Bank), Nicholas Vonortas (professor, The George Washington University), and Judy Yang (consultant, World Bank). Timothy Williams (consultant, World Bank) provided valuable research assistance and input. A background paper based on Gallup World Poll data was prepared by Leora Klapper (lead economist, World Bank) and Atisha Kumar (consultant, World Bank). A background note on the existing insolvency framework was produced by Andres Federico Martinez (private sector development specialist, World Bank), Nina Pavlova Mocheva (private sector development specialist, World Bank), Anjum Rosha (consultant, World Bank), and Mahesh Uttamchandani (lead private sector development specialist, World Bank). A box on latent entrepreneurship was prepared by Erwin R. Tiongson (senior economist, World Bank) based on ongoing work with Hilal Atasoy and others (2013), "Latent Entrepreneurship in the Europe and Central Asia Region." A background note on trade flows was produced by Giuseppe Manzillo (consultant, World Bank).

The team has greatly benefited from constructive comments from peer reviewers Mark Dutz (senior economist, World Bank), Esperanza Lasagabaster (service line manager, World Bank), Pedro Rodriguez (lead economist, World Bank) and Rashmi Shankar (lead economist, World Bank), as well as comments from Angela Prigozhina (country sector coordinator for finance and private sector in the Southern Caucasus, World Bank). The team also gratefully acknowledges the extensive comments received and incorporated from the participants at the various consultation workshops conducted in Georgia. Participants included representatives from government counterpart ministries, academics, research institutions, and the private sector. The team thanks Communication Development Inc. for valuable editing support and Paola Scalabrin and Cindy Fisher for production support of the book.

The work has been produced under the overall guidance of Henry Kerali, World Bank Country Director for Southern Caucasus; Gerardo Corrochano, World Bank Sector Director for Finance and Private Sector Development,

Europe and Central Asia Region; and Aurora Ferrari, Sector Manager, Finance and Private Sector Development, Europe and Central Asia Region. The team also gratefully acknowledges the guidance provided at the conceptualization of the study by Asad Alam, former World Bank Country Director for Southern Caucasus, and Sophie Sirtaine, former Sector Manager, Finance and Private Sector Development, Europe and Central Asia Region.

Abbreviations

ECA   Europe and Central Asia
GDP   gross domestic product
GNP   gross national product
OECD   Organisation for Economic Co-operation and Development
R&D   research and development
SMEs   small and medium enterprises

All dollar amounts are U.S. dollars unless otherwise indicated.

Overview

A dynamic and vibrant private sector is crucial to economic growth, with firms making new investments, creating jobs, improving productivity, and promoting growth. Entrepreneurial activity is pivotal to the continued dynamism of the private sector, with the generation of new businesses fostering competition and economic growth. This is particularly relevant for Georgia, whose government faces a central challenge to find sources of long-term economic growth, particularly through private sector development.

This study uses data from the new 2012 World Bank Entrepreneurship Survey conducted to gauge new firm growth in the formal sector in Georgia and data from World Bank Enterprise Surveys to analyze innovative activity in existing firms. It includes detailed case study analyses to complement these findings and to highlight the determinants of high-growth entrepreneurs.

Entrepreneurship in Georgia

Survey results indicated the following information about Georgian entrepreneurs:

- *Founder Characteristics.* The majority (62 percent) of surveyed firms had only one founder. About 20 percent of founders were women. Firms in high-tech sectors[1] had a larger share of founders with a postgraduate degree or doctoral degree. Non-high-tech firms had a larger share of founders with general management, marketing, and financial management expertise. The education level of Georgian founders was lower than that of their counterparts in Armenia, where the majority of entrepreneurs had a postgraduate degree.

- *Founders' Motivation.* The top two reasons cited for founding a business were sensing an opportunity to make more money and wanting to be one's own boss. Not finding a suitable job was cited as an important reason for starting a business by more than half of business owners in Georgia. Fearing loss of one's job was the least common reason. These patterns are in line with trends in the rest of the developing world and in Europe and Central Asia (ECA).

- *Firm Characteristics and Strategy*. The average size of surveyed firms was 12 employees. The largest firm in the sample had 220 employees. More than 90 percent of surveyed firms had no research and development (R&D) expenditures in the previous five years and did not envision spending on R&D in the next two years. This was in sharp contrast to the sample of firms surveyed in Armenia, where nearly 50 percent of surveyed firms had conducted some form of R&D in the previous five years. Almost 90 percent of firms drew funding from their founders' own savings.

- *Perceived Obstacles*. The top three cited obstacles in setting up or operating a firm were market risk/uncertainty, technological risk/uncertainty, and difficulty recruiting highly skilled employees. The most commonly cited legal and regulatory constraints were continually changing taxation regulations and high tax rates.

- *Innovative Activity*. Only 7 percent of surveyed firms indicated that they had introduced a new or substantially improved product or service in the previous three years. This was in sharp contrast with the respondents in Armenia, where 67 percent of surveyed firms indicated that they had. No products or services were new to the world in the Georgian sample, compared with 3 percent in the Armenian survey. Around 50 percent of the Georgian respondents who claimed they had introduced a new product or service said they were new to the market, compared with 80 percent of Armenian respondents.

- *Sources of Knowledge*. The most important sources of knowledge for business opportunities were clients or customers and market research from sales in the domestic market and other competitors. Universities, technical institutes, R&D firms, and external commercial labs were among the least important sources of knowledge, indicating the lack of innovative activities and industry-relevant research in these enterprises.

Policy Recommendations

The new government of Georgia has recommitted to a broad economic strategy focused on investment in the tradable sectors and export-led growth. Achieving high productivity and creating jobs are pivotal to the government's medium- to long-term goals. Fostering high-growth entrepreneurship and innovative activity is thus paramount to achieving these objectives.

Analyses in this study suggest the existence of factors that inhibit the growth of entrepreneurial and innovative activity. Further, no policies or instruments are in place to assist new entrepreneurs. The government could remove bottlenecks that impede entrepreneurialism in the general business environment and design new financial policy instruments to foster entrepreneurship and innovation. In doing so, the government needs to exercise care that the design and management of these instruments prevent capture or corruption and promote efficiency.

Increasing Access to Finance

Financial systems in Georgia are not conducive to business development. Companies cite high interest rates and risk-averse lending policies (requiring high levels of collateral) as major hindrances to expansion. In addition, risk capital is lacking. As a result of lack of borrowing opportunities, small and medium enterprises (SMEs) must rely on owners' capital or on retained earnings for investments, which greatly impedes their growth.

The government can establish favorable financing programs for SMEs by developing early-stage risk capital.

Simplifying Tax Administration

While overall tax legislation is good for firms in Georgia, its enforcement was reported to be uncertain occasionally. Individuals want more standardization and consistency in the application of laws. The tax system was dramatically simplified, with a reduction in the number of taxes from 22 to 6 in 2008. Moreover, the 2005 tax code simplified the business registration and tax payment process and reduced the number of documents required for registration. But analysis suggests that the tax code had undergone 285 changes in 2011 alone and another 135 changes by June 2012.

Greater transparency and certainty must be ensured in the tax system. The government should announce any changes to the tax code at least six months before their implementation to make it easier for firms to follow them.

Facilitating Learning from Exporting and Fostering Backward Links by Increasing Foreign Direct Investment

Openness to trade is an important source of knowledge transfer. "Learning from exporting" often takes place when exporting firms are under pressure to meet quality standards, including safety and environmental regulations, established by their customers or the regulatory authorities of destination countries. Such pressures can either strengthen incentives for exporting firms to upgrade their technology or hinder other firms that lack the requisites for exporting to more sophisticated markets.

Given the Georgian government's emphasis on export-led growth to help diversify the economy, it could focus on three priority areas:

- Introducing instruments of financial assistance to defray a portion of the cost that firms incur to acquire the requisite capacity. These could include matching grants that defray some of the costs of entering new markets through business development services.

- Providing basic infrastructure to enable firms to adhere to international standards. By building accredited control laboratories, the government could support firms in industries such as agroprocessing, which is a key priority sector for the economy and one in which adhering to global standards is a prerequisite for surviving in the global market.

- Formulating policies to promote backward links between foreign firms and the domestic economy by acting as a facilitator and gathering information on possible opportunities for links,[2] assisting in identifying partners (and arrangements) by matching suppliers' capabilities and buyers' needs (legal assistance, fairs, missions, conferences and exhibitions, and so forth), and providing economic incentives in the form of tax exemptions and subsidies to promote training and technology transfer from buyer firms to local supplier firms.[3]

Developing Skills

Stakeholders repeatedly cited inadequate skills as a key hindrance to developing local industry. While the majority of the population has higher education, their skills are not aligned with industry needs, thus indicating a skills mismatch. In particular, both technical and managerial skills are lacking. This reflects the course curriculum's strong focus on theory, containing little practical education and being almost fully removed from the market. Improving the quality and industry relevance of education needs to be an important component of the government's agenda to improve competitiveness.

Medium- to long-term policies need to reorient the higher education system to produce more industry-relevant skills. Firms in Georgia could also benefit from training and mentoring graduates straight out of school. One such measure is Singapore's SME Talent Program, which allows SMEs to sponsor study awards to qualified students of the institutes of technical education and polytechnics, followed by a job offer upon graduation. By attracting and nurturing talent, the program helps SMEs build a strong labor core.

In addition, more emphasis is needed on industry-relevant vocational training and education courses that cater to the technical needs of the various priority sectors identified by the government. In this process, a feedback mechanism between firms and the government is necessary, with feedback being provided to the design and development of new courses that respond to the skills needs of industry.

Increasing Industry-Research Collaboration and In-Firm R&D

There is virtually no industry-research collaboration in Georgia. Furthermore, R&D is limited, even among the high-growth firms. Synergies need to be built between the industry and research communities, and firms must be incentivized to conduct more in-house R&D.

The government can provide incentives for industry and researchers to effectively collaborate. Technology transfer organizations can facilitate knowledge transfer from research institutions to SMEs through collaborative research and technology programs as well as through staff exchanges and secondments (placing researchers and engineers in firms). Furthermore, enhancing in-house R&D capabilities is fundamental. *The government should introduce policy instruments that foster R&D and innovation in the private sector, including direct funding (grants and subsidies), matching grants, and R&D tax credits.*

Facilitating Firm Exit and Restructuring

Lowering barriers to exit and enabling restructuring of viable firms are important means of fostering entrepreneurship. "Insolvency" in Georgia is defined as the inability of the debtor to pay its debts as they become due. It is thus possible that a viable business with cash flow problems may be pronounced insolvent and forced into bankruptcy. To rehabilitate a business that is insolvent but remains viable, additional loans may be required.

The insolvency law should be changed to include incentives that motivate the banking sector to provide post-petition financing.

For an insolvency regime to be effective, it must be accessible to all stakeholders. In Georgia it is difficult for a creditor to initiate insolvency proceedings. A creditor seeking to force a debtor into bankruptcy must either show two valid court decisions against the debtor for nonpayment of dues or hold a substantial percentage of the insolvent debtor's debt. This dampens the confidence that creditors have in loan recovery, making them more risk-averse.

Creditors should be allowed to initiate insolvency proceedings to increase their confidence in loan recovery, thus making them less risk-averse to lending.

Raising Awareness

Governments elsewhere have also played a key role in raising awareness of the private benefits of undertaking entrepreneurial activities. In the United Kingdom in 1979, the government's idea was to change the social attitudes of the U.K. population away from what the government perceived as a "dependency culture," in which workers relied on large organizations and the state for employment, to an attitude among individuals of striving to start their own businesses and creating an "enterprise culture."

School curriculum in Georgia needs to factor in prerequisites that encourage innovative thinking. Showcasing successful entrepreneurs could go a long way in fostering the entrepreneurship culture in society.

Summary of Policy Recommendations and Timelines

Policy measure	Timeline
Improving efficiency in business environment	
Announce any changes to the tax code at least six months before their implementation to make it easier for firms to follow them.	0–3 months
Increased access to finance	
Establish favorable financing programs for SMEs by developing early-stage risk capital.	6–12 months

table continues next page

Summary of Policy Recommendations and Timelines *(continued)*

Policy measure	*Timeline*
Increased access to markets	
Introduce instruments of financial assistance to defray a portion of the cost that firms incur to acquire the requisite capacity to complete on the global market (for example, matching grants to buy business development services).	6–12 months
Provide basic infrastructure to enable firms to adhere to international standards by building accredited control laboratories.	Greater than 1 year
Formulate policies to promote backward links between foreign firms and the domestic economy.	3–6 months
Developing skills	
Reorient higher education programs to produce more industry-relevant skills.	Greater than 1 year
Emphasize industry-relevant vocational training and education courses that cater to the technical needs of the various priority sectors identified by the government.	6–12 months
Increasing firm-level R&D and industry-research linkages	
Introduce programs and policies that encourage R&D in firms (for example, R&D tax credits and matching grants).	3–6 months
Introduce programs and policies that incentivize industry and researchers to effectively collaborate.	3–6 months
Facilitating firm exit and restructuring	
Change the insolvency law to include incentives that motivate the banking sector to provide post-petition financing.	6–12 months
Allow creditors to initiate insolvency proceedings.	6–12 months
Raising awareness	
Change the school curricula to encourage innovative thinking.	6–12 months
Increase awareness of entrepreneurship by showcasing successful entrepreneurs.	0–3 months

Notes

1. Chemical industry, manufacture of basic pharmaceutical products, manufacture of computer and other electronic equipment, manufacture of electrical equipment, and information and communication.

2. Either directly or by supporting private institutions, governments promote the creation of information exchanges that could range from lists of inputs and materials available locally—which might include prices and qualities—to names, locations, and profiles of local suppliers.

3. By exempting exporters from value added tax, governments encourage the use of local inputs; by treating costs incurred in the creation of links as tax-deductible expenses from corporate income tax, governments promote their creation.

CHAPTER 1

What Drives Entrepreneurship and Economic Growth?

Job creation and productivity growth are at the forefront of today's global development agenda. The 2013 World Development Report on jobs identified entrepreneurship as an important tool in addressing these dual goals.

Increased productivity occurs due to the reallocation of new products and services entering markets toward profitable uses. The Organisation for Economic Co-operation and Development (OECD)–Eurostat Entrepreneurship Indicator Program (2009) established the following definitions building on past theoretical contributions in the literature (OECD 2009):

- *Entrepreneurs* are those persons (business owners) who seek to generate value through the creation or expansion of economic activity by identifying and exploiting new products, processes, or markets. Job creation and productivity growth are at the forefront of today's global development agenda. The 2013 World Development Report on jobs identified entrepreneurship as an important tool in addressing these dual goals.
- *Entrepreneurial activity* is an enterprising human action in pursuit of the generation of value through the creation or expansion of economic activity by identifying and exploiting new products, processes, or markets.
- *Entrepreneurship* is the phenomenon associated with entrepreneurial activity.

These definitions take into consideration several important issues. First, by distinguishing between entrepreneurs and entrepreneurial activity, these definitions recognize that while entrepreneurs engage in entrepreneurial activity, such activity does not necessarily require the actions of entrepreneurs. That is to say, the definitions recognize the possibility of entrepreneurial activity within extant businesses by individuals who do not have a stake in the company (employees). Second, not all businesses—in fact, not all new businesses—are entrepreneurial in the sense of identifying or creating new products, processes, or markets. Third, rather than concentrating on entrepreneurial individuals or companies that succeed, the definitions broaden the scope of analysis to those

Figure 1.1 Conceptual Framework

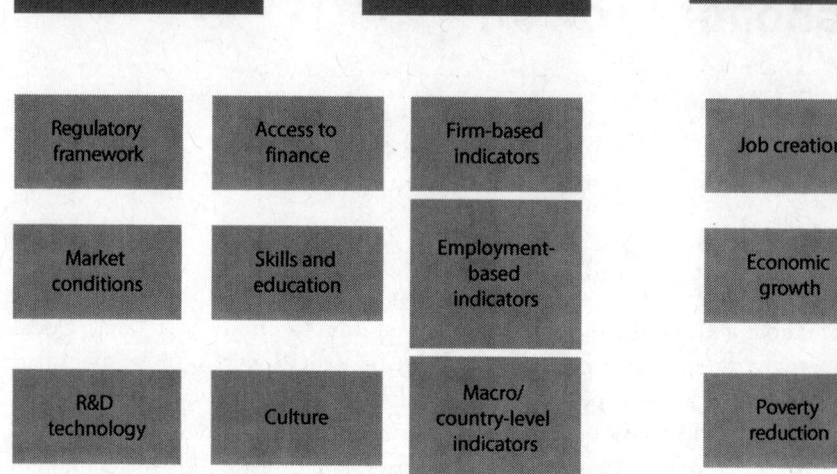

Source: OECD 2009 with some modifications.
Note: R&D = research and development.

that seek to generate value through such activity. Fourth, the notion of value is left open in order to include the traditional objective of economic growth as well as other objectives such as increasing employment, decreasing inequality, and tackling environmental problems. But the importance of entrepreneurship goes beyond firm entry and relates to the introduction of new products and process innovation, which enables firms to enter new markets.

This study uses the entrepreneurship model put forth in the OECD-Eurostat Entrepreneurship Indicator Program (2009), with minor modifications (figure 1.1). The model comprises various determinants that policy can affect and that in turn influence entrepreneurial performance, or the amount and type of entrepreneurship that take place. The model then refers to the impact of entrepreneurship on higher-level goals such as economic growth, job creation, and poverty reduction. This study focuses on determining the level of entrepreneurship in Georgia and analyzes the role of each determinant in both fostering and constraining entrepreneurial activity.

Motivations for Entrepreneurs

Entrepreneurs view opportunities in the economy by measuring their profit-making potential; that is their first motivation. Entrepreneurs will not pursue a societal need unless they can successfully make a profit. They are motivated by the accumulation of wealth but also by the need to achieve (Shane, Locke, and Collins 2003). Despite being risk takers, they may not seek out the riskiest opportunities, but they are willing to take on some risk. Entrepreneurs evaluate opportunities in the marketplace differently depending on how they perceive the level of risk and assess the capacity for mitigating it. Several external factors influence the level of risk, such as environmental regulations, political attitudes, industry regulation, industry health, state of technology, market size, and availability of resources, including venture capital and skilled labor (Hayter 2011).

Entrepreneurs may be pushed into self-employment and starting a business by necessity—that is, the lack of other employment options and the need for income. Alternatively, they may be pulled into starting a business because they recognize opportunities and choose to pursue them. Necessity-driven entrepreneurship is expected to be more prevalent in less developed and developing (factor-driven) economies. The importance of necessity as a motivator gradually decreases with greater economic development, while that of opportunity increases (Kelley, Singer, and Herrington 2012).

Determinants of Entrepreneurship

As the conceptual framework in figure 1.1 shows, a host of factors determine the propensity of an individual or a firm to engage in entrepreneurial activities. It must be recognized at the outset that the determinants highlighted in this framework are in no way independent of each other.

The overall regulatory framework encompasses numerous elements, including the number of days required to start a business, insolvency and bankruptcy laws that determine firm survival and exit, and factors such as the extent of red tape. The overall regulatory framework thus impacts both firm entry and firm exit. Klapper and Love (2012) analyzed the World Bank Entrepreneurship database (World Bank 2008a), which collects data on total and newly registered businesses in more than 100 industrial and developing countries. Their analysis shows that a strong business and regulatory environment can encourage entrepreneurial activity. Capture and corruption also determine the level of productive entrepreneurial activity, as they directly influence the expected payoffs associated with undertaking entrepreneurial activities.

Lowering bankruptcy costs is another important step in enabling new firms to enter the market, especially in industries with naturally high entry rates (Klapper, Laeven, and Rajan 2006). Bankruptcy law and reform deeply affect entrepreneurs who are subjected to external risks when starting and running their businesses. An effective bankruptcy system can provide the possibility of a "fresh start" if the first effort fails and can limit entrepreneurs' losses in bankruptcy. A forgiving personal bankruptcy law and ready availability of limited liability can stimulate entry by "latent" entrepreneurs who would otherwise be too risk-averse to start their own business (Armour and Cumming 2008). Countries with high or unlimited exemptions in personal bankruptcy law attract 25 percent more entrepreneurial activity than those with low exemptions (Fan and White 2003; Mathur 2009), although increasing the cost of credit (Berkowitz and White 2002).

Access to finance is an important determinant of innovative activity for both new and existing firms. Impediments to accessing finance are often larger for small and medium enterprises (SMEs) and stem partly from the demand side of financial markets. Credit is more readily available to businesses that have immovable property (land and buildings) to be used as collateral than to those having movable assets, as banks strongly prefer immovable property to secure a loan. Insufficient suitable collateral is often cited among the top reasons for difficulty accessing credit, especially for small firms. Other obstacles to expanding access to finance include insufficient or inadequate financial and other information on SMEs available to bankers, who therefore find it difficult to make an informed credit decision. In addition to finance from banks, venture capitalists and angel investors can foster entrepreneurial activity.

Market conditions, which are determined largely by the overall regulatory framework, include such factors as the level of competition in factor and product markets. Market structure and competition are likely to affect a firm's ability to innovate or undertake other entrepreneurial activities. In theory the relationship between competition and innovation by incumbent firms is ambiguous (Aghion and others 2005). On the one hand, firms that are far behind the technological frontier may reduce investment in innovation in the face of competition from new entrants, because innovation is very costly to them and competition would erode rents obtained from innovating. On the other hand, firms that are close to the technological frontier need to spend relatively little to stay ahead of new entrants; competition, therefore, would create greater incentives for them to spend on innovation. The level of competition is in turn influenced by an economy's openness to trade and foreign direct investment, which increase exposure to foreign competition and induce the adoption of more advanced technologies in both export- and import-competing firms (see Schiff and Wang 2006). Furthermore, participation in export markets enables firms to become more productive, a phenomenon referred to as "learning through exporting." Firms can absorb technology by exporting to customers who will provide signals in meeting standards and requirements to access global markets. Lederman (2009), using firm-level data from enterprise surveys in several countries, finds that a firm's exporting status (that is, whether it exports more than 10 percent of its sales) is positively correlated with the probability that it innovates. Historical accounts of the rise of East Asian export industries stress the role of advanced country buyers as conduits of technological and managerial know-how to developing country firms (Pack and Westphal 1986).

Research and development (R&D) capacity is a crucial determinant of a firm's ability to innovate. Lederman (2009), using firm-level data, finds evidence that R&D is significantly and positively correlated with the probability that a firm innovates. R&D has a role in developing a firm's ability to identify, assimilate, and exploit knowledge from the environment—that is, to enhance the entrepreneurial capacity of the economy. Here it is important to employ a broad definition of R&D: the inclusion of improvements in existing processes or products as well as the imitation and adoption of knowledge. Hence R&D is not restricted to original innovation. While R&D investment oriented toward "new-to-the-world" innovations predominates in developed economies, developing economies need R&D to be able to absorb new technologies and keep up with existing global technological trends, a phenomenon that Cohen and Levinthal (1989) refer to as the "second face of R&D."

A vital determinant of entrepreneurial activity is the accumulation of human capital and the skill level of the workforce. An educated workforce can be considered a precondition for a country to have the capacity for knowledge acquisition and adaptation, especially in an environment in which firms face competitive pressures that call for frequent changes in product mix and production technology (Kuriakose, Goldberg, and Zhang 2011). In addition to education levels, evidence suggests a relationship between the level of training and technological adaptation. Higher levels of training and skills typically lead firms to identify new technologies that need to be mastered to increase competitiveness. Yet a firm's decision to acquire a certain technical competency often necessitates training and changes in the workforce's skill composition. For example, training in Russian enterprises is highly correlated with indicators of innovativeness such as R&D or licensing of patents and know-how, introduction of new production technologies, and high-technology exports (Tan and others 2007). The diaspora and other networks can serve as a source of skills, entrepreneurial ability, and business and marketing expertise. Diaspora can also contribute to entrepreneurship by strengthening trade and investment links (World Bank 2008b).

Entrepreneurship also depends on various *social and individual characteristics* of gender and culture. It involves taking risks, and potential entrepreneurs cannot be risk-averse. The recent European Bank for Reconstruction and Development's (2011) *Life in Transition Report* suggests that despite the fact that women in transition economies have similar levels of education, training, and skills as men, they are less likely to become entrepreneurs, with one of the reasons cited being the fact that women are more risk-averse.

Rather than an inborn skill, entrepreneurship is largely a product of environment. It involves a complex of economic and social behaviors. Entrepreneurship can flourish only in the right environment. Social values, culture, government policies, the political system, technology, economic conditions, customs, and laws influence entrepreneurship. Iyer and Schoar (2010) explored the importance of culture in determining contractual outcomes through field experiments in India and found that entrepreneurs from different communities vary in how they conduct business and negotiate contracts.

Cultural values deeply affect entrepreneurship and economic development. Culture affects the entrepreneurial process and focuses on the discovery and interpretation of opportunities. It trains people along particular lines. It nurtures enterprising and risk-bearing behavior. Starting with Max Weber, sociologists have argued that entrepreneurship is most likely to emerge in a specific social culture. According to them, social sanctions, cultural values, and role expectations are responsible for the emergence of entrepreneurship. Some cultures are enormously supportive of entrepreneurship. Others may not regard it so favorably. These differences go a long way toward explaining why some societies are vibrant and progressive and others stagnate.

High-Growth Entrepreneurship

An important distinguishing factor among SMEs is their rate of growth. The OECD defines "high-growth enterprises" as firms that have annualized growth in number of employees above 20 percent over a three-year period and have at least 10 employees at the beginning of the measurement period (OECD 2009). Analysts see high-growth enterprises as a source of entrepreneurial vitality that are promoted as important drivers of economic growth and job creation. An especially important subset of high-growth enterprises is firms that are less than five years old. These young high-growth firms—often referred to as "gazelles"—account for less than 1 percent of all firms in most countries throughout the world, but are responsible for a much larger percentage of new jobs and economic growth.

Recent studies have alerted policymakers to the importance of high-growth firms as job creators. Henrekson and Johansson's (2010) review of the literature finds that, despite many differences in measures of growth, time periods, industries, firm sizes, firm ages, methods of analysis, and geographical coverage, there is agreement on several facts:

- A few rapidly growing firms—gazelles—generate a disproportionately large share of all new net jobs compared with non-high-growth firms. This is more pronounced in a recession, when gazelles continue to grow.
- Gazelles tend to be younger than average. Age seems to be the most important differentiating factor, more important than size.
- Gazelles are of all sizes. Small firms dominate in terms of numbers but larger gazelles are important contributors of jobs, especially a small subgroup called supergazelles. Supergazelles are both large firms and major net job creators.
- Gazelles are spread over all industries. They are not overrepresented in high-technology sectors as is sometimes hypothesized. If anything, they appear to be overrepresented in service sectors.

Regarding the "mice against gazelles" debate—whether the entry of many new firms (mice) or the rapid growth of a few firms (gazelles) generates employment growth—the literature suggests that the two views are complementary. The continuous entry of new firms is required for net job creation. The evidence indicates that a high inflow of new firms increases the likelihood of generating young gazelles, which tend to contribute more to employment than do older gazelles.

Finally, Henrekson and Johansson (2010) argue strongly that net employment growth must be viewed in the perspective of Schumpeterian creative destruction, in which net employment growth is the result of considerable churning and restructuring in a dynamic process of firm entry, expansion, decline, and exit. While some firms may be more important than others in creative destruction, a prerequisite for their growth is that creative destruction works so that efficient, new, and expanding firms attract resources from inefficient firms released through contraction and exit. In other words, turbulence in the sense of firm entry and exit is necessary to boost job creation. An employment-enhancing policy should lower the barriers for firm entry and exit, thus supporting the experimental process that allows repeated trials and increases the chances of establishing new gazelles.

Role of Government

A fundamental question stemming from analyzing these determinants of entrepreneurship is how to design effective public policy that promotes innovative firm creation and enables existing firms to catch up, improve productivity, and grow. Experiences from Asian countries and developed economies have shown that innovative SMEs and knowledge-based firm creation have played a major role in the development of new national economic advantages. In this context public policy is pivotal in creating an enabling environment that helps alleviate the market failures that inhibit firm growth.

Emerging markets have other environmental conditions that are not present (or are less prevalent) in developed markets, and investors considering investing in emerging markets will face added risk as a result. Given the increased risk (or even uncertainty) that investors may face when taking a stake in a company in an emerging market, the government may need to intervene by subsidizing financing or by absorbing some of the investment risk. Its possible actions include:

- Supporting companies at the seed stage, when market-based mechanisms for funding tend to fail.
- Mitigating the costs of failure so that entrepreneurs can recover from a failed business.
- Ensuring that everyone plays by the same rules.
- Training competent business managers and tying government support to requirements for monitoring and management assistance.
- Being selective and using meritocratic criteria in choosing which companies to fund.
- Systematizing seed and venture capital financing.

References

Aghion, P., N. Bloom, R. Blundell, R. Griffith, and P. Howitt. 2005. "Competition and Innovation: An Inverted U Relationship." *Quarterly Journal of Economics* 120 (2): 701–28.

Armour, J., and D. Cumming 2008. "Bankruptcy Law and Entrepreneurship." *American Law and Economics Review* 10 (2): 303–50.

Berkowitz, J., and M. J. White. 2002. "Bankruptcy and Small Firms' Access to Credit." Working Paper w9010, National Bureau of Economic Research, Cambridge, MA. http://ssrn.com/abstract=316789.

Cohen, W, and D. Levinthal. 1989. "Innovation and Learning: the Two Faces of R&D." *Economic Journal* 99 (397): 569–96.

EBRD (European Bank for Reconstruction and Development). 2011. *Life in Transition Report*. London: EBRD.

Fan, W., and M. J. White. 2003. "Personal Bankruptcy and the Level of Entrepreneurial Activity." Working Paper w9340, National Bureau of Economic Research, Cambridge, MA. http://ssrn.com/abstract=351432.

Hayter, C. S. 2011. *What Drives an Academic Entrepreneur?* New York: New York Academy of Sciences.

Henrekson, M., and D. Johansson. 2010. "Gazelles as Job Creators: A Survey and Interpretation of the Evidence." *Small Business Economics* 35 (2): 227–44.

Iyer, R., and A. Schoar. 2010. "Are There Cultural Determinants of Entrepreneurship?" In *International Differences in Entrepreneurship*, edited by J. Lerner and A. Schoar, 209–40. Chicago, IL: University of Chicago Press.

Kelley, D. J., S. Singer, and M. Herrington. 2012. *Global Entrepreneurship Monitor: 2011 Global Report*. London: Global Entrepreneurship Research Association.

Klapper, L., L. Laeven, and R. Rajan. 2006. "Entry Regulation as a Barrier to Entrepreneurship." *Journal of Financial Economics* 82 (3): 591–629.

Klapper, L., and I. Love. 2012. "The Impact of Business Environment Reforms on New Firm Registration." Policy Research Paper 5493, World Bank, Washington, DC.

Kuriakose, S., I. Goldberg, and C. Zhang. 2011. *Fostering Technology Absorption in Southern African Enterprises*. Washington, DC: World Bank.

Lederman, D. 2009. "The Business of Product Innovation: International Empirical Evidence." Policy Research Working Paper 4840, World Bank, Washington, DC.

Mathur, A. 2009. "A Spatial Model of the Impact of Bankruptcy Law on Entrepreneurship." *Spatial Economic Analysis* 4 (1): 25–51.

OECD (Organisation for Economic Co-operation and Development). 2009. *Measuring Entrepreneurship: A Collection of Indicators 2009*. Paris: OECD.

Pack, H., and L. Westphal. 1986. "Industrial Strategy and Technological Change." *Journal of Development Economics* 22 (1): 87–128.

Schiff, M., and Y. Wang. 2006. "North-South and South-South Trade Related Technology Diffusion: An Industry Level Analysis of Direct and Indirect Effects." *Canadian Journal of Economics* 39 (3): 831–44.

Shane, S., E. A. Locke, and C. J. Collins. 2003. "Entrepreneurial Motivation." *Human Resource Management Review* 13 (2): 257–79.

Tan, H., Y. Savchenko, V. Gimpelson, R. Kapelyushnikov, and A. Lukyanova. 2007. "Skills Shortages and Training in Russian Enterprises." Policy Research Working Paper 4222, World Bank, Washington, DC.

World Bank. 2008a. Entrepreneurship (database). http://econ.worldbank.org/WBSITE/ EXTERNAL/EXTDEC/EXTRESEARCH/EXTPROGRAMS/EXTFINRES/0,, contentMDK:21454009~pagePK:64168182~piPK:64168060~theSite PK:478060,00.html.

———. 2008b. *Global Economic Prospects: Technology Diffusion in the Developing World*. Washington, DC: World Bank.

———. 2013. *World Development Report: Jobs*. Washington DC.

CHAPTER 2

Georgia's Economic Structure and the Role of Entrepreneurship

Motivation

The central challenge today for the government of Georgia is to find sources of long-term economic growth, particularly through private sector development. The enterprise sector is heavily dominated by retail and other sectors that do not generate opportunities for increased trade or value added production (figure 2.1). Continued growth will require not only higher savings and investment, but also a serious refocusing on domestic production, with an emphasis on productivity enhancements and diversification. In particular, Georgia will need to focus on supporting exports, with particular attention to improving competitiveness in the manufacturing and agriculture sectors, to spur economic growth.

Recent Economic Performance

Trade Structure

Georgia has a trade–to–gross domestic product (GDP) ratio, fluctuating between 60 percent and 70 percent over 2003–11 and revealing a high openness to trade. However, trade is driven primarily by the nontradable sector, and thus Georgia lags behind regional peers in exports. Moreover, the export product mix has become increasingly concentrated, indicating a pressing need to diversify. The top eight export products of 2011 accounted for 67 percent of exports in 2005 and 78 percent in 2011. During this time the export of repaired and remanufactured vehicles increased considerably, from 3 percent in 2005 to 23 percent in 2011.

Shares of nonoil commodities and high-tech products in the export composition have increased over the last decade (figure 2.2; see appendix B for a description of categories). Top exports in 2011 included petroleum oils (27.7 percent of total exports), ferro-silico-manganese (11.5 percent), copper ores and concentrates (10.3 percent), ammonium nitrate (5.9 percent), hazelnuts or filberts (4.2 percent), and wine and grape must with ferment (1.7 percent) (UN 2013). Exports of services were heavily concentrated in transportation and

Figure 2.1 Enterprise Sector Breakdown, 2012

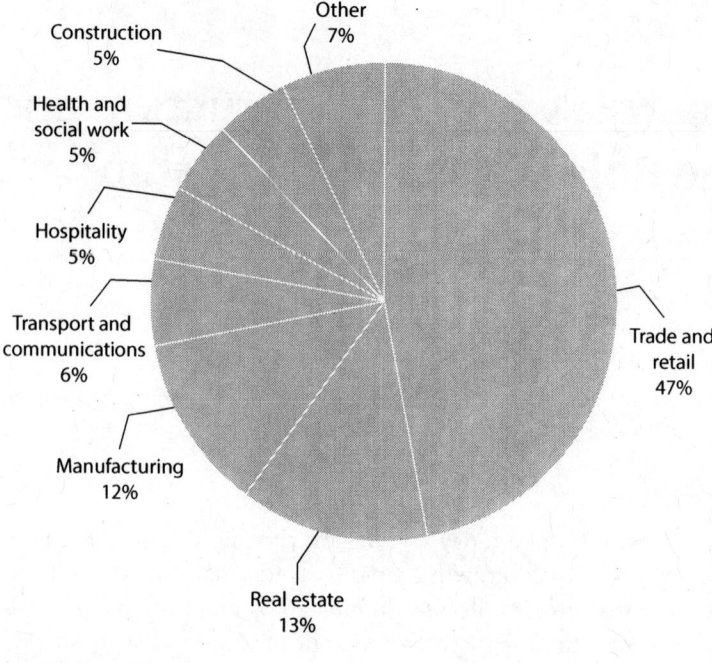

Source: GeoStat 2012.

travel, which together accounted for 85 percent of total services exports in 2010 (figure 2.3).

Employment

Though unemployment has declined slightly as Georgia recovers from the global economic crisis, it remains higher (15.1 percent in 2011) than in many of its neighboring countries and higher than the Europe and Central Asia (ECA) average of around 7 percent (figure 2.4). Among the unemployed, younger people are impacted the most (figure 2.5). Formal employment accounts for about 30 percent of the labor force, and self-employment accounts for about 64 percent (mainly in rural areas and agriculture), reflecting the primarily subsistence nature of the Georgian economy.

Many of the unemployed are highly educated, with almost half having tertiary education, indicating a substantial skills gap and a need for greater alignment between the education system and the needs of the private sector.

Despite noticeable improvement over the last decade, Georgia has one of the largest informal sectors in the region. In 2002 Georgia had the largest informal sector (67.3 percent of gross national product [GNP]) of 23 European transition economies (which averaged 38 percent; Schneider 2002). Since then, the informal sector has shrunk considerably, to an estimated 22 percent of GDP in 2010 (OECD 2012). The drop was a result of strong economic growth combined

Figure 2.2 Composition of Exports by Level of Technology, 1994–2011

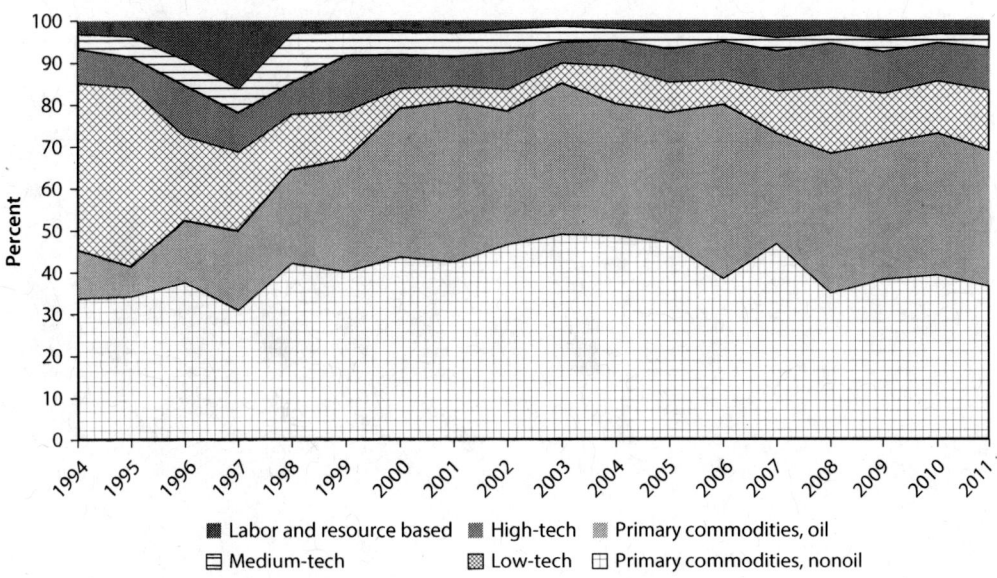

Legend:
- ■ Labor and resource based
- ⊟ Medium-tech
- ▨ High-tech
- ▩ Low-tech
- ▨ Primary commodities, oil
- ⊡ Primary commodities, nonoil

Source: United Nations Comtrade database 2013.

Figure 2.3 Exports of Services, 2010

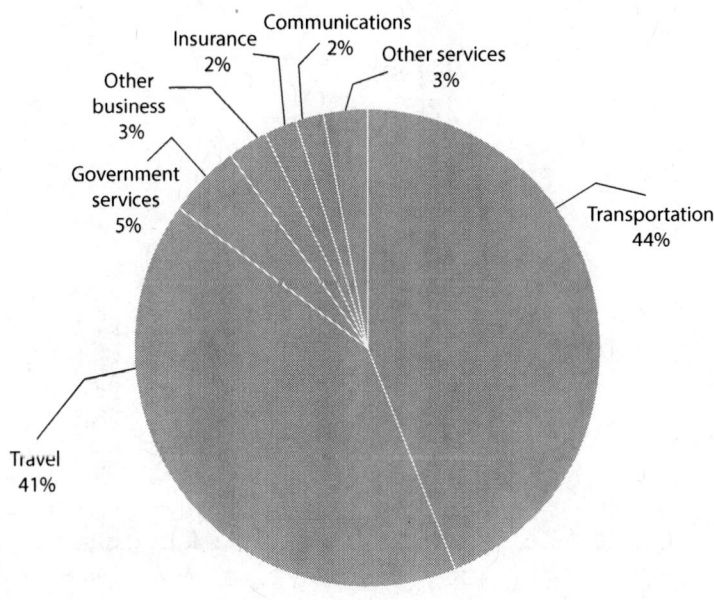

Communications 2%
Insurance 2%
Other services 3%
Other business 3%
Government services 5%
Transportation 44%
Travel 41%

Source: United Nations Service Trade Database 2012.

Fostering Entrepreneurship in Georgia • http://dx.doi.org/10.1596/978-1-4648-0062-7

Figure 2.4 Unemployment Rates by Country, 2011

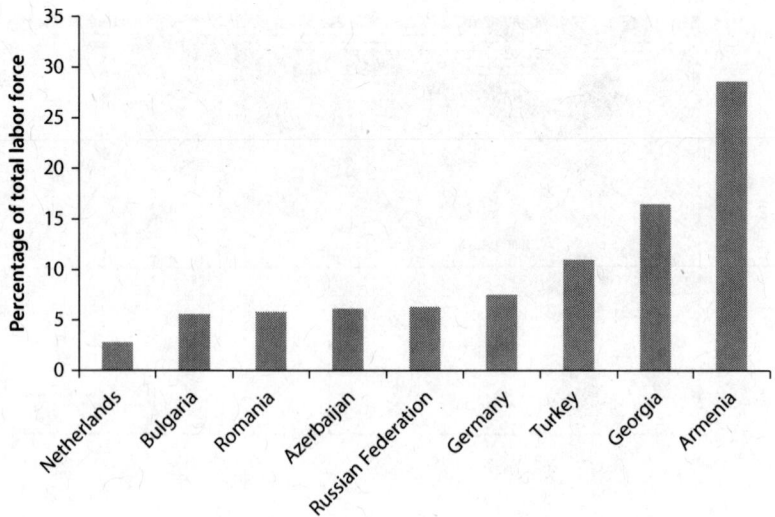

Source: World Bank 2013.

Figure 2.5 Unemployment by Age, 2011

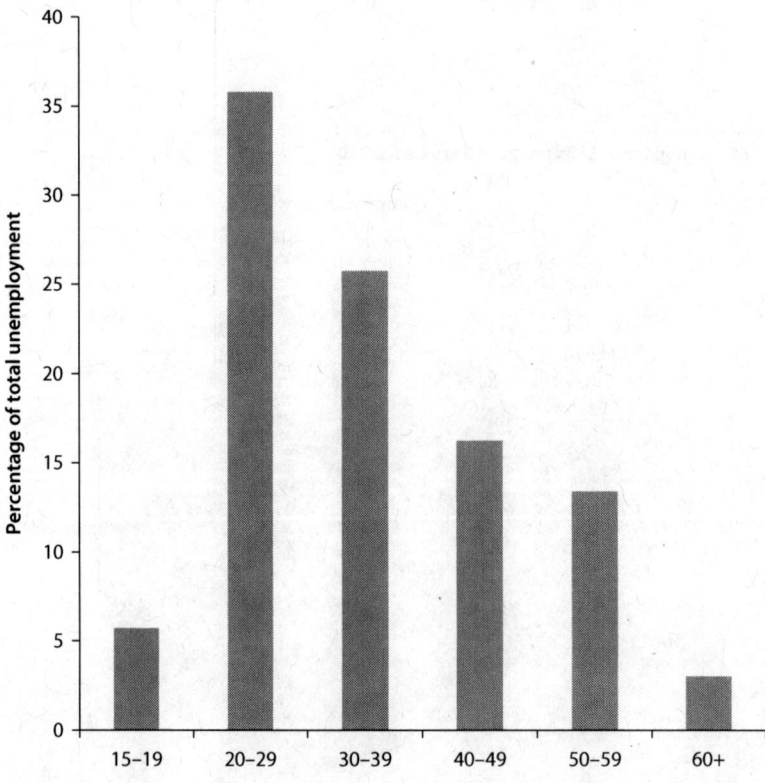

Source: GeoStat 2012.

with policies to reduce regulatory and fiscal burdens on firms. Regardless, informality in the economy remains high, particularly in the construction and services sectors. Christie (2008) found that nonobserved activities[1] accounted for 32 percent of output in the construction sector, 94 percent in repair services, and 87 percent in the restaurant and bar sectors.

Small and medium enterprises (SMEs) account for a large share of the Georgian enterprise sector: 90 percent of firms, representing 38.1 percent of salaried employees.[2] Moreover, the number of small firms is continuously increasing, at an estimated 15 percent a year, while medium-size and large firms are shrinking. This is likely an effect of the large shadow economy in the country. Countries with a large shadow economy typically show a scarcity of new medium-size and large firms and an excess of small and relatively inefficient firms, which would have disappeared or been forced to improve in the absence of the shadow economy (Christie 2008). Several of these SMEs are inactive and make limited economic contributions. SMEs accounted for only 19.3 percent of value added in 2010 and 14.4 percent of turnover in 2011 (OECD 2012).

An entrepreneurial mindset exists in Georgia. A large share of Georgia's employed population is self-employed. Over the last five years self-employment has remained roughly 62 percent of total employment.[3] However, self-employment skews largely to older populations (figure 2.6). In addition, self-employment positions are mostly subsistence living or in the informal sector. There is little evidence of high-growth entrepreneurship in the country.

A 2011 nonrepresentative survey showed that Georgians have a strong entrepreneurial spirit. Some 92 percent of surveyed individuals said they would like to be self-employed, and roughly 51 percent believed it would be feasible to become self-employed in the next five years, indicating that there exists both an

Figure 2.6 Self-Employment by Age, 2011

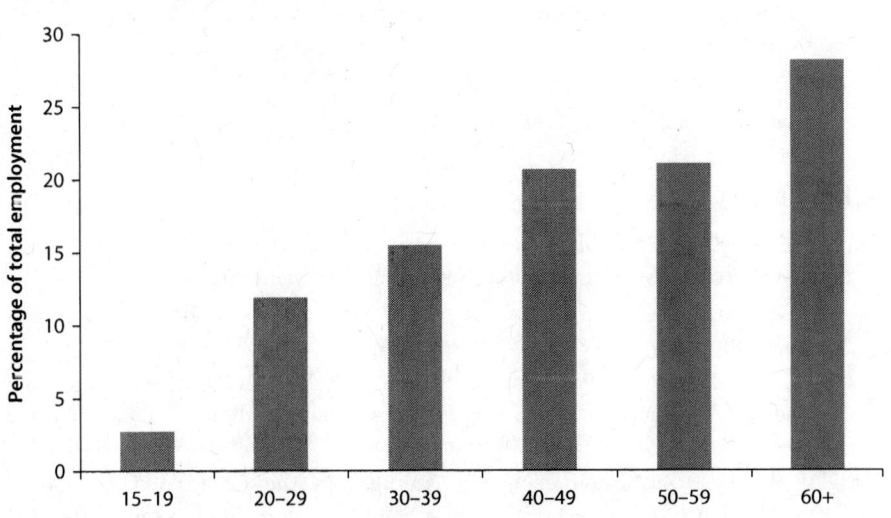

Source: Geostat 2012.

Fostering Entrepreneurship in Georgia • http://dx.doi.org/10.1596/978-1-4648-0062-7

interest in entrepreneurship and a confidence in the reforms and stability of the country (Natsvlishvili 2011).

It is possible to encourage small business development and growth by tapping into the entrepreneurial potential and mindset prevalent in Georgia. Encouraging high-growth entrepreneurship can help Georgia as it moves toward new opportunities in value added and tradable sectors.

Empirical Analysis

This study analyzes both entrepreneurial activity by individuals (measured by the creation of a new legal entity in the formal sector) and entrepreneurial activity by existing firms (measured by the introduction of new products or new processes or by entrance into new export markets).

For entrepreneurial activity by existing firms, the study looks at "new-to-the-world" innovative activity, which is the development and commercialization of new unproven technologies and untested processes and products, and "new to the country/market" innovative activity, which is the application of existing technologies, processes, and products in a new environment in which the processes have not yet been tested and the markets and commercial applications are not fully known. For developing countries, most technological progress is likely to originate from the adoption of technologies first discovered elsewhere, with firms adapting these to local market conditions, rather than by introducing new-to-the-world technologies (Goldberg and others 2008).

Notes

1. The nonobserved economy encompasses all productive economic activity that was not observed by the National Statistics Agency, including the shadow economy (defined as legal and productive economic activities that are partially or completely concealed from authorities to avoid compliance with taxes and regulations), informal sector production, production of households for their own final use, and illegal production.

2. http://www.investingeorgia.org.

3. Geostat data from 2005 to 2011.

References

Christie, E. 2008. *The Non-Observed Economy in Georgia: Economic Analysis and Policy Recommendations*. New York: United Nations Development Programme.

GeoStat (Georgia Department of Statistics). 2012. "Main Statistics". http://www.geostat .ge/index.php?action=page&p_id=116&lang=eng.

Goldberg, I., L. Branstetter, J. G. Goddard, and S. Kuriakose. 2008. "Globalization and Technology Absorption in Europe and Central Asia: The Role of Trade, FDI and Cross-Border Knowledge Flows." Working Paper 150, World Bank, Washington, DC.

Natsvlishvili, I. 2011. "Entrepreneurship Attitudes in the Context of Post-Soviet Transformation (Case of Georgia)." Tbilisi State University and George Washington University, Washington, DC.

OECD (Organisation for Economic Co-operation and Development). 2012. *SME Policy Index: Eastern Partner Countries 2012: Progress in the Implementation of the Small Business Act for Europe.* Paris: OECD.

Schneider, F. 2002. "Size and Measurement of the Informal Economy in 110 Countries around the World." Presented at a workshop of Australian National Tax Centers, Australian National University, Canberra, July 16. http://rru.worldbank.org/Documents/PapersLinks/informal_economy.pdf.

UN (United Nations). 2012. UN Service Trade (database). https://unstats.un.org/unsd/servicetrade/default.aspx.

———. 2013. "Commodity Trade Statistics Database (Comtrade)." http://comtrade.un.org.

World Bank. 2013. *World Development Indicators 2013.* Washington, DC.

CHAPTER 3

Entrepreneurship and New Firm Growth

This chapter describes entrepreneurial activity by individuals as measured by the creation of a new legal entity in the formal sector. The analysis uses an existing dataset, the Gallup World Poll Dataset, and a new survey covering 300 entrepreneurs[1], which was conducted specifically for this study. In addition, case studies highlight the evolution of many entrepreneurial endeavors and the characteristics important in the formation of these enterprises and their subsequent growth.

Entrepreneurship Landscape

Firm Entry Density

The World Bank Entrepreneurship database provides data on formal firm entry density. "Entry density" is the number of newly registered companies per 1,000 working-age (ages 15–64) population. The database does not account for informal firms and measures only private, formal companies with limited liability. Firm entry density varies across Armenia, Azerbaijan, Georgia, and Europe and Central Asia (ECA) as a whole. Georgia stands out with a mostly increasing trend over time, sharply since 2009 and well above the ECA average since 2007 (figure 3.1). Entry density in Armenia and Azerbaijan remains below the ECA average.

General Trends in Entrepreneurship

Despite the high entry density, firm ownership in Georgia remains lower than the ECA and developing country averages. According to the 2011 Gallup World Poll[1], 15 percent of individuals in developing countries reported owning a business, compared with 6 percent in ECA, 2 percent in Armenia, 5 percent in Azerbaijan, and 4 percent in Georgia (figure 3.2). One potential reason for the discrepancy between the high business entry rate and the low business ownership rate could be the different sample of firms: the Gallup World Poll data cover firms in the informal sector while the Entrepreneurship database looks only at formally registered firms.

Figure 3.1 Firm Entry Density for ECA and Southern Caucasus Countries, 2012

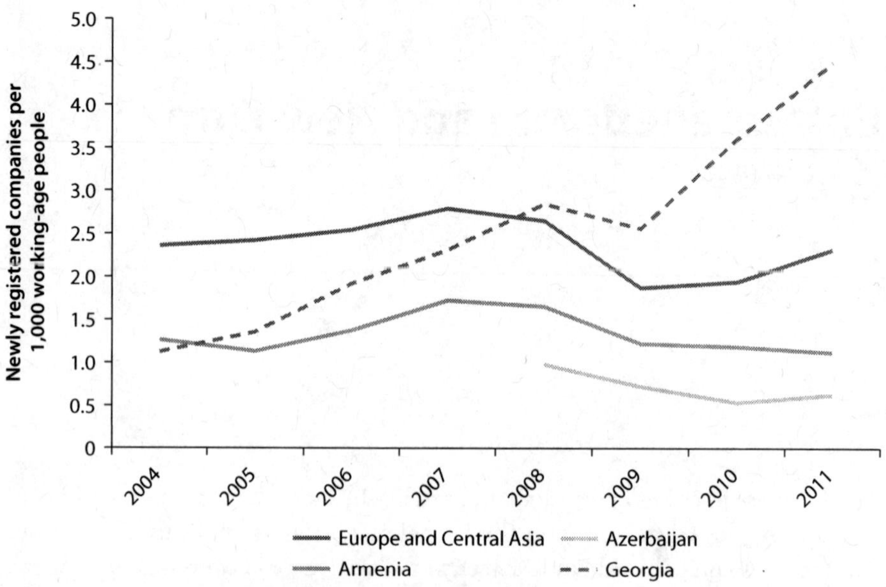

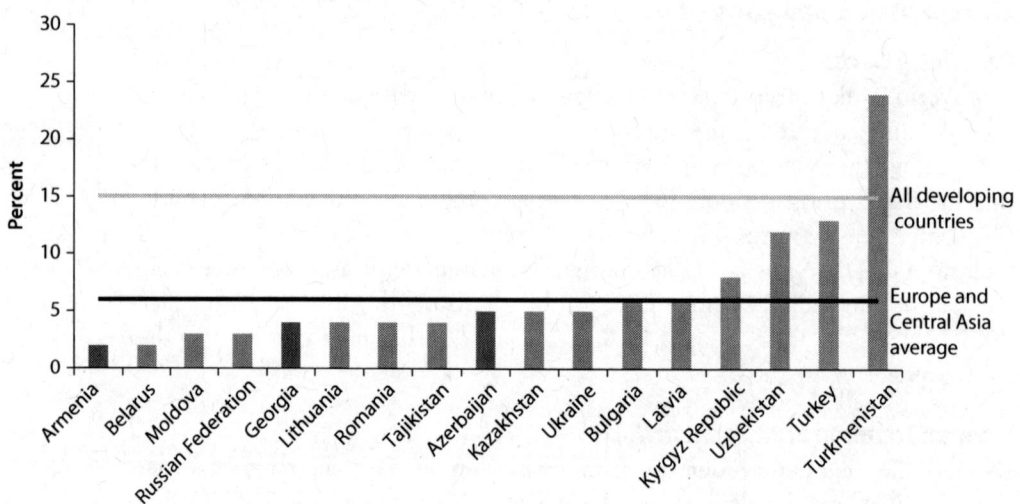

Source: World Bank Entrepreneurship database 2012a.
Note: Entry density for Europe and Central Asia (ECA) is calculated with population-weighted averages for working-age (ages 15–64) population, using data from World Bank (2013). Averages are based on countries with full data coverage for 2004–11.

Figure 3.2 Business Ownership in Europe and Central Asia, 2011

Source: Gallup World Poll 2011.

Latent Entrepreneurship

Another measure of interest is the pool of potential entrepreneurs known as "latent entrepreneurs"—those who are not actual entrepreneurs but want to be.[2] Data from the 2010 Life in Transition Survey is used to analyze this pool of entrepreneurs.

Georgia compares unfavorably with other ECA countries. Only about 12 percent of the labor force and about 10 percent of the wage-employed can be considered latent entrepreneurs, far below the ECA average of 27 percent of the labor force and 22 percent of those wage-employed. It also lags behind Armenia, though it compares favorably with Azerbaijan.

Econometric analysis of latent entrepreneurs suggests that a few individual characteristics are important[3]: women are less likely to be latent entrepreneurs, consistent with gender patterns of actual entrepreneurial activities. Among men, latent entrepreneurs tend to be married and have larger households, which suggests that preference for self-employment may partly reflect a desire for the greater flexibility afforded by entrepreneurship and self-employment. At the same time, higher per capita income, which may serve as a proxy for wealth, is associated with a greater likelihood of latent entrepreneurship, consistent with the literature. The literature on entrepreneurship has explained low rates of entrepreneurship as a function of social values and attitudinal characteristics, and at least one dimension of trust (trust in foreign investors) is strongly related to latent entrepreneurship for the sample as a whole and for the separate samples of men and women. But trust in people is a statistically significant correlate of latent entrepreneurship only among women. Meanwhile, there are no discernible statistical links with educational attainment.

The 2010 Life in Transition Survey data also provide information on previous attempts to start a business. In Georgia, close to fifth of the labor force and the wage employed previously tried to start a business, slightly more than the regional average. And of those who attempted to start a business, about half succeeded, less than the ECA average (about two-thirds) but more than in Armenia and Azerbaijan.

The correlates of such successful attempts are instructive: per capita income and general satisfaction with one's financial situation again play a role. Access to finance—as proxied by being able to borrow money—is a statistically significant correlate of successful business startups. Interestingly, although women are less likely to be latent entrepreneurs, when they attempt to start a business, they are just as likely to succeed as men are.

Survey Results

This section is based on the 2012 World Bank Entrepreneurship Survey, which was conducted for this study and is complemented by the findings from the Gallup Survey where relevant. The new survey aimed to capture the sources of financing, education levels of the owners and managers of firms, the business environment constraints that firms face, and whether firms have used government programs to help startup and growth. The sample of surveyed firms consisted of 300 firms between 2 and 10 years old.

Founder Characteristics

Some 62 percent of surveyed firms had only one founder (11 percent had three, and 5 percent had four; figure 3.3). Only about 18 percent of founders

Figure 3.3 Gender and Number of Founders in Sample

Source: World Bank Entrepreneurship Survey for Georgia 2012b.

Figure 3.4 Education Levels of Founders, by Sector

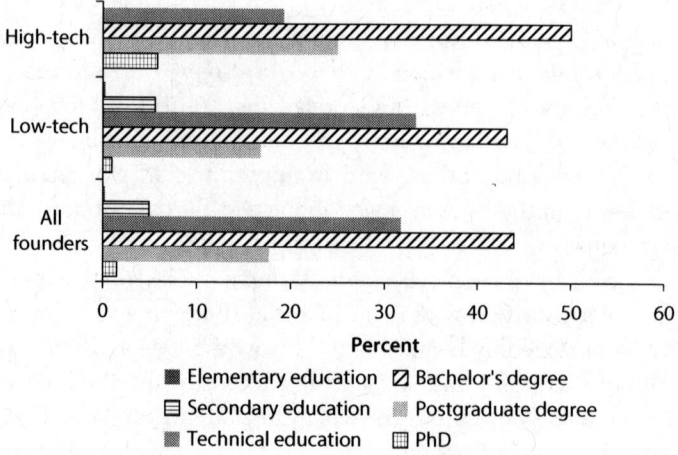

Source: World Bank Entrepreneurship Survey for Georgia 2012b.

were women. According to the Global Entrepreneurship Monitor (2011), the ratio of female to male entrepreneurs varies considerably across the global sample: from 1:5 in the Republic of Korea to 6:5 in Ghana. The report also finds that, across the 59 economies studied, only one economy, namely Ghana, had proportionately more women than men entrepreneurs, and only a handful had equal proportions of women and men. The vast majority of economies had more men than women entrepreneurs. The most common education level among Georgian firm founders was a bachelor's degree (44 percent), followed by technical education (32 percent). Firms in high-tech sectors[4] had a larger share of founders with a postgraduate degree or doctoral degree (figure 3.4). All founders in high-tech sector firms had at least a technical education. By contrast, non-high-tech firms had a larger share of founders with general management, marketing, and finance expertise.

The education level of Georgian entrepreneurs was lower than that of their counterparts in Armenia, where the majority of the entrepreneurs had a postgraduate degree. Most of the surveyed entrepreneurs in Georgia had worked in the same industry in which they founded their new firm. Founders averaged of six years of experience in the same sector, less than in both Armenia and Azerbaijan (nine years). Nearly 40 percent of founders were more than 40 years old, older than the global average. Georgian entrepreneurs who founded high-tech firms were generally younger, with nearly 20 percent of these high-tech founders ages 18–29.

Founders' Motivation

The Gallup World Poll asked business owners why they started a business. Business owners in Georgia reported the top two reasons as sensing an opportunity to make more money and wanting to be one's own boss (figure 3.5).

Figure 3.5 Reasons for Starting a Business

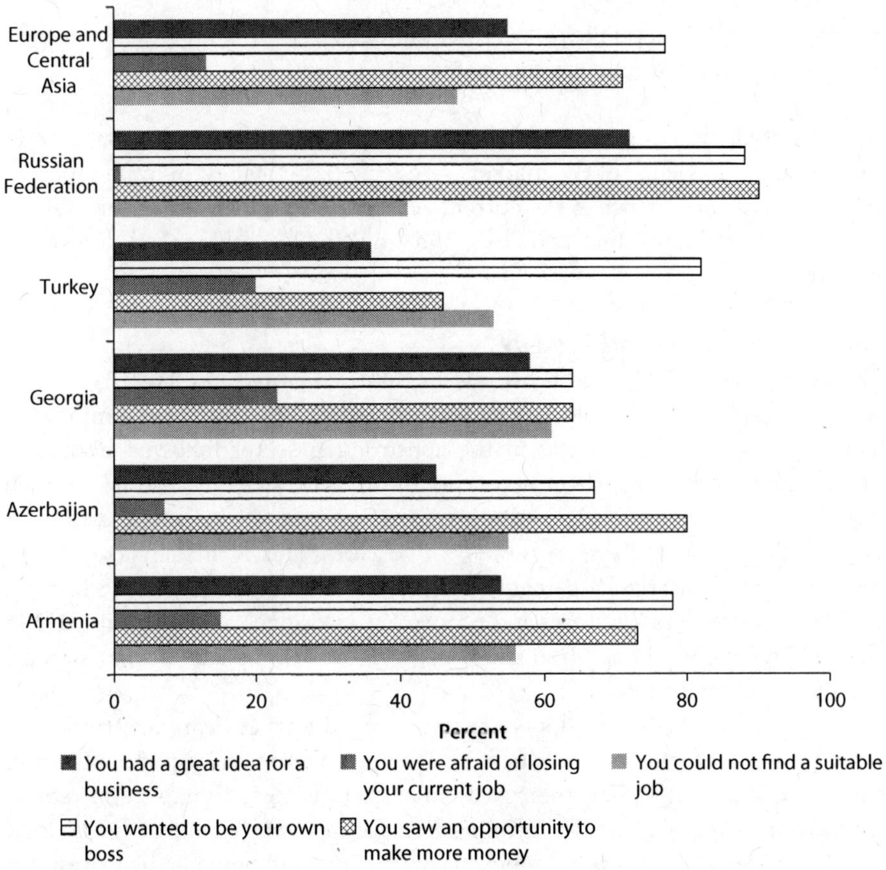

Source: Gallup World Poll 2011.

Not finding a suitable job was cited by more than 50 percent of business owners. Fearing loss of one's job was the least common reason. These patterns are in line with trends in the rest of the developing world and in ECA. The desire to be self-employed is not driven by necessity or at least not by necessity alone (so-called survival entrepreneurship). In fact, many of those already in the labor force or already wage-employed prefer to run their own business. The survey data also show that men are considerably more likely than women to cite wanting to be their own boss as an important reason for starting a business. Respondents with tertiary education or higher are more likely than those with secondary education to cite having a great idea for a business.

The World Bank Entrepreneurship Survey asked entrepreneurs to cite the importance of the following factors in the formation of their company:

- Work experience in the current activity field.
- Technical/engineering knowledge in the field.
- Design and software knowledge.
- Knowledge of the market.
- Availability of finance.
- Networks built during previous career.
- Opportunities in a public procurement initiative.
- Existence of a large enough customer base.

In Georgia the existence of a large enough customer base, availability of finance, and knowledge of the market were ranked the highest in importance. In Armenia work experience in the current activity field, knowledge of the market, and technical/engineering knowledge in the field were ranked the most important.

Firm Characteristics and Strategy

The average size of surveyed firms was 12 full-time employees. The largest firm in the sample had 220 employees, and 64 percent had fewer than 10 employees. The largest share of firms was in the construction sector followed by freight services and hotels. More than 90 percent of the firms surveyed had no research and development (R&D) expenditures in the previous five years and did not envision spending on R&D in the next two years. This is in sharp contrast to Armenia, where nearly 50 percent of surveyed firms conducted some form of R&D in the previous five years and 55 percent envisioned spending on R&D in the next two years. Some 96 of the firms were new firms and did not spin off from a larger parent firm.

The vast majority of products or services produced at firm inception were modifications of existing products or services. Georgian respondents were four times less likely than their Armenian counterparts to engage in radical innovations that were new to the market. Almost 90 percent of firms drew funding from their founders' own savings; only 20 percent also drew on funds from banks (see box 3.1). Firms that spin out of a preexisting

Box 3.1 Case Study: JSC Margebeli—The Role of a Philanthropic Angel Investor

General information about the founder and formation

JSC Margebeli was founded by Michael Margebeli and a friend and cofounder (a Swiss doctor) in 1997 when they met during a trip the doctor made to the Georgian countryside. A rapidly developing friendship and trust emerged, which led to the doctor offering $40,000 to help establish Healthy Water, the first company of the group. The company produces natural mineral water in the village Nabeghlavi. The Swiss investor essentially became its foreign business angel investor and helped it repeatedly. He has invested about $1 million in the company over the years. In return he has 50 percent ownership.

Company strategy. The company started with five people in the mineral water business and has now expanded to 600 full-time employees and a wide range of products. Five years ago it went into agriculture and food processing. To accomplish high-quality production, Margebeli uses sophisticated techniques and trains workers. It also imports highly qualified personnel to run the business. Two highly qualified German engineers head the production facility in food processing, and two qualified Swiss agroengineers manage agricultural production.

In 2003 the factory at Nabeghlavi was fully modernized, and the company reportedly increased production dramatically. For this modernization the company obtained German equipment with funding from Switzerland and the Georgian Development Bank. Ten years later it operates what is reported to be an ultramodern bottling facility with a production capacity of 30,000 bottles per hour.

Margebeli already has a very large share of the Georgian market in water (55 percent) and strong shares in processed foods. It is actively trying to export to countries of the former Soviet bloc, such as Kazakhstan, Turkmenistan, and Ukraine, as well as the United States. To generate such business, the founder regularly visits international exhibitions.

About 50 percent of the employees have a higher education degree. In addition, the company provides on-the-job training. It also brings foreign experts to train employees in house and places a high value on learning form international experiences. But finding workers remains difficult, particularly ones who are willing to work at odd hours, since the company runs 24 hours a day.

Innovation and business models. The company is relentlessly innovating by adding new varieties of processed foods, diversifying business horizontally (from mineral water to food processing) and vertically (from food processing to agriculture). There is a specific focus on producing high-quality products with the best production techniques. Mr. Margebeli stresses incorporating new production techniques, acquiring top-of-the-line machinery, and hiring excellent personnel.

Perceived role of the government. Mr. Margebeli thinks that the country sorely lacks a good agriculture school and that one is needed, which would focus heavily on practical education and would train people in modern agricultural techniques. This school should benefit from international teachers.

Figure 3.6 Percentage of Adults Who Reported Saving

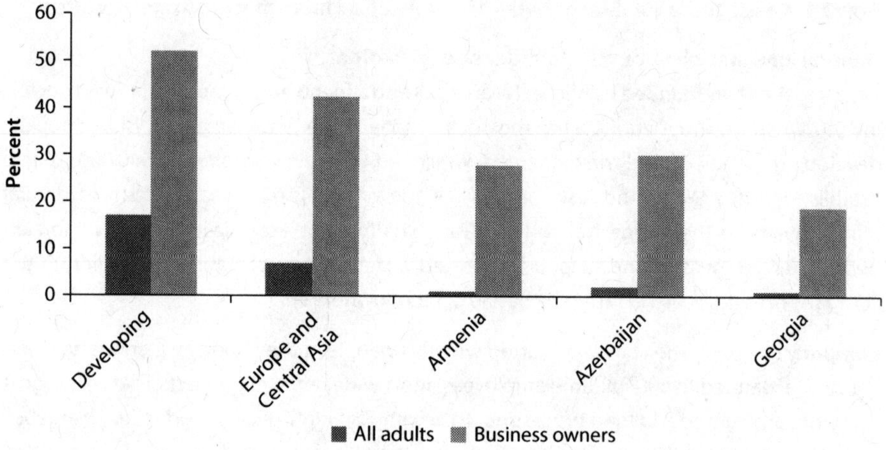

Source: Gallup World Poll 2011.

organization had easier access to external sources of funding—implying easier access to finance for preestablished firms. Business owners have higher levels of savings than the adult population as a whole (figure 3.6), which is in line with findings from the Entrepreneurship Survey, in which a majority of founders financed their entrepreneurial activity using their own savings.

The most important factors for firms to maintain their competitive advantages were capability to offer high-quality products/services, capacity to adapt products/services, and capability to offer novel products/services (figure 3.7; see boxes 3.2, 3.3 and 3.4). The least important factors cited were marketing and promotion activities and undertaking R&D. Further, Georgian respondents pursue a price-based competition in standardized markets, which is in contrast with their Armenian counterparts, who are more aggressive in searching for niche markets by producing unique products through greater R&D investments.

Market Environment

Two-thirds of surveyed firms cited having many business competitors. Overall, Georgian respondents reported higher levels of competition than their Armenian counterparts. This could reflect the fact that Georgian entrepreneurs are making products that are slight modifications of existing products, implying that there would be more Georgian firms selling very similar products. By contrast, Armenian firms spend more on R&D, trying more innovative products to differentiate themselves from potential competitors. More than 90 percent of surveyed firms in Georgia sell to the local/regional market (figure 3.8). These businesses sell about 75 percent of their products to the local/regional market. Only 11 percent of businesses sell internationally. However, these businesses sell nearly half their products internationally (figure 3.9). Overall, Georgian

Figure 3.7 Contribution in Creating and Sustaining the Competitive Advantage of the Company

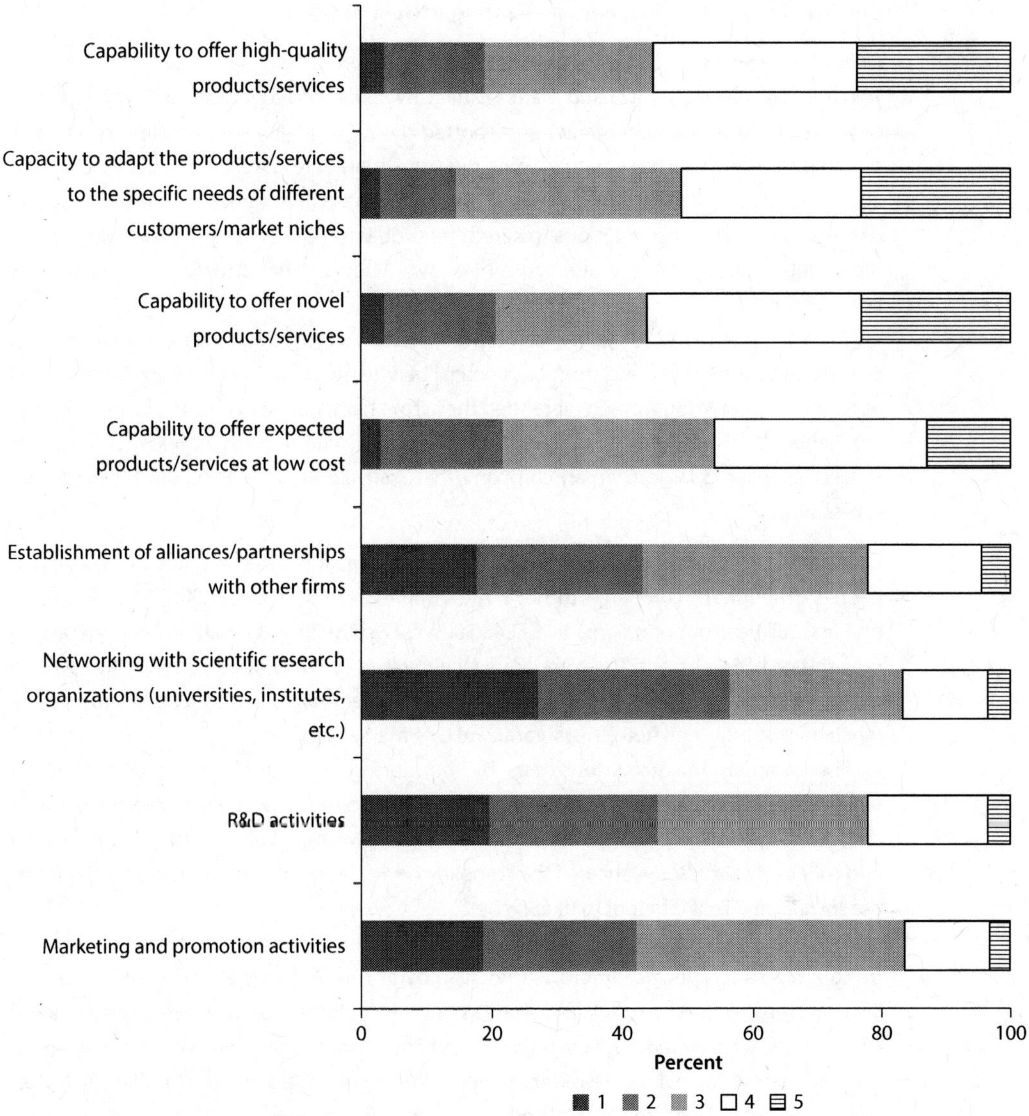

Source: World Bank Entrepreneurship Survey for Georgia 2012b.
Note: R&D = research and development. 1 = no impact; 5 = huge impact.

small companies seem more oriented to local and regional sales than their Armenian counterparts. The Armenian small companies are more open to national and international sales.

Perceived Obstacles
Entrepreneurial activity requires a degree of risk taking due to uncertainties. To obtain insights into the perceived obstacles facing entrepreneurs, the survey

Box 3.2 Case Study: Tea Mania—Finding a Niche Market

General information about the founder and formation

Two friends, Eka Verulashvili and Marika Bibileishvili, decided to look for a novelty product or service for the Georgian market and spotted the high-quality specialty tea market for a possible new venture. The young women did some market research and in 2006 decided to start a franchise of a Russian company, Untsia. The franchise signed a one-year contract before Georgian-Russian relationships became problematic, resulting first in cancelation of direct flights between the two countries and later in the disruption of diplomatic relationships.

The startup required $30,000, which came from their supportive families, since loans without any substantive collateral from commercial banks had very high interest rates. After two years of operations, the women rebranded their store name to Tea Mania and started working independently from the Russian franchise. They established a direct business contact with Untsia's supplier, a large German company that sold high-quality tea, coffee, sweets, and accessories.[a]

Company strategy and business model. Tea Mania remains a small business, employing 15 people, although the company's turnover grew impressively from GEL84,000 ($51,000) in 2007 (the first full year of operations) to GEL450,000 ($275,000) in 2011, with an average annual growth rate of 56 percent. The company's strategy is to grow by opening new elite specialty tea stores in prestige locations or shopping malls that generate big traffic and by entering the medium- and high-end hotel, restaurant, and café market segment.

The company maintains low costs by introducing lean management and computer technologies in accounting, thus keeping administration costs low, and simplifying supply chain management by having only one large supplier of the main products. Diversification into coffee and accessories showed the company could be flexible, adapting its product mix to the specific needs of different market niches.

Tea Mania used the shop-in-a-shop concept, since it knew that Georgians would not go to a tea shop specifically but would stop by at one if they were in a shopping mall. This strategy helped attract Tea Mania's initial customer base. Having well trained consultants, who were knowledgeable about the numerous varieties of tea, was one of the key factors in making Tea Mania successful in selling its tea and coffee to hotels, restaurants, and cafés. Tea Mania's unique selling proposition was that customers could buy tea in very small quantities from a big array of choices. High-quality Georgian products, like handmade tea and honey, became a new addition to their product mix and a new attraction for customers. Today the company is present in more than 25 high-end restaurants and cafés in Tbilisi and Batumi, and it has plans to expand into Armenia.

In 2010 the young women spotted a good opportunity for forward integration into a restaurant business by opening a restaurant, Downtown, which, just like Tea Mania, became a brand name as well.

box continues next page

Box 3.2 Case Study: Tea Mania—Finding a Niche Market *(continued)*

Perceived role of the government. Tea Mania participated in a business advisory services program financed by the European Bank for Reconstruction and Development and fully enjoyed the benefits of having a marketing consultant in the company. It has not received any support from the government. However, it has highlighted two important areas for government focus: the vocational training of restaurant personnel, which would push the development of the hospitality sector in Georgia, and simplification of tax administration at the border for small businesses.

a. The German supplier sources the tea from various parts of the world such as India and Sri Lanka.

Box 3.3 Case Study: Pro-Service—Finding an Underserved Market

General information about the founder and formation
In 2003 George Natroshvili, an engineer, was looking for a provider of web-hosting services but found none in Georgia. With an avid interest in information technology, he identified a new business opportunity. His brother Rezo, a sales manager in a Coca-Cola factory in Georgia, became his partner, and they founded Pro-Service. The startup required a small amount of funding (about $10,000), which the brothers were able to finance by themselves. The first product they offered was website design. In 2004–05 they developed the search engine "boom.ge" for the Georgian market. The company started to sell advertising space for clients, which was a novelty at the time. Its product did not generate much income but gave them high visibility and recognition.

Market environment. Although the information and communication technology sector is still early in its development, the demand for web hosting and web-based applications has greatly improved. In 2007 the company started to offer web-hosting services, including shared hosting, a virtual dedicated server, and a dedicated server with 24/7 support. It started to target the higher price segment of the market and to offer packages with high-quality services. It offered much lower prices on web hosting than Caucasus Online. This, in combination with server renting and virtual servers (which other companies could not offer), gave Pro-Service a competitive advantage. Currently it hosts 4,067 web pages and claims to have up to 40 percent of the market, positioning it as the second-largest company in web hosting after Caucasus Online. The third line of business is the boom.ge search engine, which hosts client advertisements. Web hosting accounts for about 80 percent of the company's income. Website design accounts for the rest.

Company strategy, innovation, and business model. The company grew 10–15 percent a year over 2003–11, increasing its staff from 5 to 21 employees and raising sales to $500,000 in 2011. The company's main challenge is to develop a sustainable growth strategy on the market with underdeveloped demand and limited resources in software engineers. Its business model is to be a specialized niche company in web hosting and web applications that provides high-quality services and after-sale support.

box continues next page

Box 3.3 Case Study: Pro-Service—Finding an Underserved Market *(continued)*

Pro-Service sees its strengths as excellent sales skills, highly qualified support staff, and high-quality website design, with the added bonus of a reliable content management system. The firm provides a lifetime warranty, providing around-the-clock support to clients if they experience problems. In addition, it continuously updates features, creating new designs every year, though existing clients must pay for new features. It retains highly qualified staff by paying a good salary, since getting skilled personnel is often difficult.

Internationalization and export of its services are Pro-Service's growth strategies. It has sold its services in Latvia. In addition, it has recently opened a subsidiary company in Armenia, Serveam, where it will offer the same web-hosting services to clients with good support in the Armenian language. The services will be provided from Georgia and do not require additional investments in Armenia.

International competition exists in the form of major web-hosting providers like GoDaddy. Pro-Service differentiates its offerings from GoDaddy's: while GoDaddy offers unlimited space for $10 a month, Pro-Service offers limited space for $4 a month under the realization that most companies do not need unlimited space.

The next probable step will be to open a dedicated data center, which does not yet exist in Georgia. Currently Pro-Service buys servers and rents space on them to its clients. But it is reaching the physical limits of the storage space for its servers. The planned data center will host a large numbers of servers in one location with state-of-the-art conditions. In addition to its own servers, the data center will host the servers of client companies. The projected ideal size of the data center is 200 square meters, and the cost will be $5 million.

Figure 3.8 Market Distribution of Sales

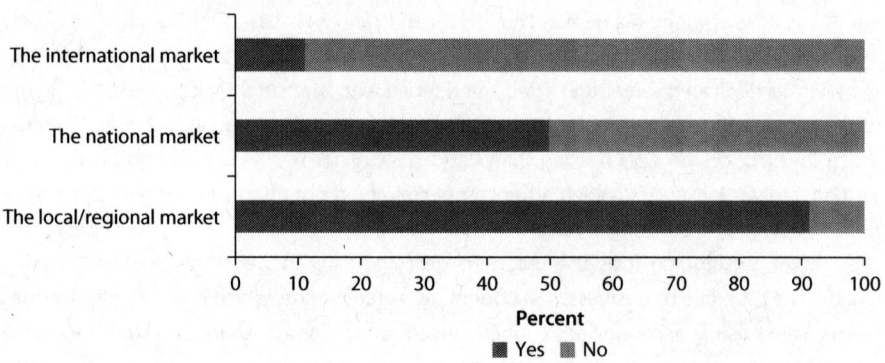

Source: World Bank Entrepreneurship Survey for Georgia 2012b.

asked respondents to rate whether the following factors were obstacles in setting up or operating a firm:

- Technology risk/uncertainty.
- Market risk/uncertainty.
- A large initial investment.

Figure 3.9 Share of Total Sales When Product Is Sold to Market Type

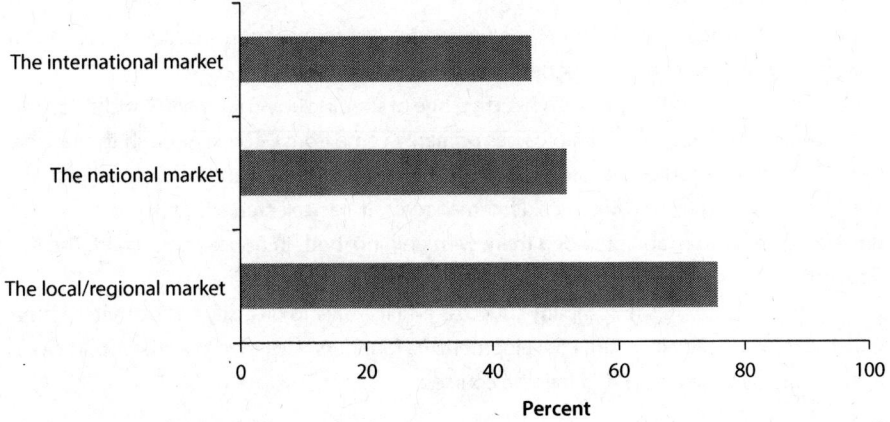

Source: World Bank Entrepreneurship Survey for Georgia 2012b.

Box 3.4 Case Study: Palitra Media—Continuously Diversifying into New Products

General information about the founders and formation process

Palitra Media was founded in 1995 by entrepreneur Irakli Tevdorashvili and two of his friends. The three were working together in a printing house when they decided to set up their own business. They pooled their money and invested roughly $300 to purchase a large supply of paper. Once they had generated some capital, they expanded their business to act as an intermediary between clients and the printing press. In 1995 they purchased a printing house that had gone bankrupt and started taking orders.

At that time, there was only one other large competitor in the market, a state-owned printing house. Palitra was able to fill an existing gap in the printing business, which was known for producing additional copies without the author/publisher being aware, selling these hidden copies, and misappropriating income. Palitra's key value proposition when it entered the market was that not one copy would be lost in printing; thus it earned the trust of many clients. It was able to attract *Seven Days*, a popular newspaper, away from the state-run printing house, which was its first order. Shortly thereafter, it began publishing its first newspaper.

Company strategy. Today Palitra has expanded into a multimedia company, working in several media platforms including print media, FM radio broadcasts, and Internet TV. This has resulted in its expansion in 17 years from 10 employees to more than 1,000, with 500 in the publishing operations, including newsroom, editorial staff, and journalists; 150 in the printing house; and 150 in the network of stores and distributors. In addition, Palitra has an advertising company that sells advertising space to Georgian firms, a press distribution agency, a book publishing house, and more than 20 bookstores throughout the country.

In 2005 Palitra established a news agency, InterPressNews, which functions around the clock and provides information in three languages—Georgian, Russian, and English.

box continues next page

Box 3.4   Case Study: Palitra Media—Continuously Diversifying into New Products *(continued)*

In print media, the company publishes around 20 newspapers and magazines. Its weekly newspaper *Kviris Palitra* has the highest circulation in the country.

As it has grown, the company has hired a range of staff, including journalists, technical staff, and creative designers. The workforce has primarily come from Georgia, though the firm has recently started outsourcing some work to Ukraine (web designers) and India (programmers). The firm has had difficulty finding skilled managers. It has selected students from the best universities in Georgia and provided them with training, both in-house and abroad. The firm does not maintain a full-time training budget but trains according to need.

A key contributor to the company's success and its drive to diversify has been its international links. Since early in Palitra's development, its founders have tried to actively participate in international conferences and training courses.

Innovation and business models. Recognizing that the world is focusing on mobile media platforms, the company has created the first Georgian newspaper application for Apple devices. The *Kviris Palitra* application is available for iPhone, iPad, and iPod touch in both the Russian and English languages. To cater to customer needs, the group made the application multifunctional, allowing readers to download the newspaper, see photos, and read the paper offline. The *Georgian Journal* will also be available shortly, both on the Apple and Android platforms.

- Difficulty finding the necessary funding.
- Difficulty finding business partners.
- Difficulty recruiting highly skilled employees.
- Lack of technological know-how.

In Georgia the top three cited obstacles were market risk/uncertainty, technological risk/uncertainty, and difficulty recruiting highly skilled employees. In Armenia the top three cited obstacles were difficulty recruiting highly skilled employees, market risk/uncertainty, and difficulty finding the necessary funding. In Azerbaijan the top three cited obstacles were difficulty finding the necessary funding, large initial investment, and difficulty finding business partners.

The survey also asked respondents about their perceived legal and regulatory constraints, which included

- Continually changing taxation regulations.
- High tax rates.
- Time-consuming regulatory requirements for issuing permits and licenses.
- Poorly enforced competition law to curb monopolistic practices.
- Poorly enforced property rights and copyright and patent protection.
- Strict property, copyright, and patent protection.
- Government officials favoring well connected individuals.
- Bankruptcy legislation making the cost of failure immense.
- Rigid labor market legislation.

In Georgia the most commonly cited constraints included continually changing taxation regulations and high tax rates. Analysis conducted by GeoWel Research found as many as 285 amendments to the tax code in 2011, reflecting the continually changing taxation regulations that businesses would find difficult to keep track of. Continually changing tax regulations is the most cited constraint for both Armenian and Azerbaijani respondents as well, with the additional constraint of government officials favoring well connected individuals in Armenia, and bankruptcy legislation making the cost of failure immense in Azerbaijan.

Innovative Activity

To gauge the level of innovative activity by businesses, the survey asked respondents whether they had introduced a new or substantially improved product or service in the previous three years. Only 7 percent of the Georgian respondents indicated that they had, compared with two-thirds of Armenian respondents. No products or services were new to the world in the Georgian sample, compared with 3 percent in the Armenian sample, and around 50 percent of products or services were new to the market in Georgian sample, compared with more than 80 percent in the Armenian sample.

In Georgia the main objective of introducing a new product or service was to increase domestic sales in market segments in which the firm was already operating and to diversify its product mix for the domestic market. The most common area for introduction of new products or services was in methods of manufacturing, and the least common area was logistics, supply chain, and delivery or distribution methods for inputs, products, or services.

The most important sources of knowledge for new business opportunities are clients or customers and market research through sales in the domestic market and other competitors (figure 3.10). Universities, technical institutes, R&D firms, and external commercial labs are among the least important sources of knowledge, indicating both the nature of innovative activities in these enterprises and the lack of industry-relevant information from research and training institutions. This was further corroborated in the detailed case studies. Industry-relevant skills are not available, and little R&D is conducted, even in high-growth firms.

Testing Hypotheses

Using the survey data collected from each of the three countries, two models were used to understand the relationship between firm growth and various founder and market characteristics. The first model used an ordinary least squares regression to look at the determinants of firm growth as measured by average sales growth during the previous five years (see box C.1 for details of the specification).

The following hypotheses were tested:

H1: Younger, smaller firms grow faster.
H2: Founders' expertise at company setup is very important for firm growth. Prior experience in industry, especially in the same sector, positively affects

Figure 3.10 Importance of the Following Sources of Knowledge for Exploring New Business Opportunities for the Company

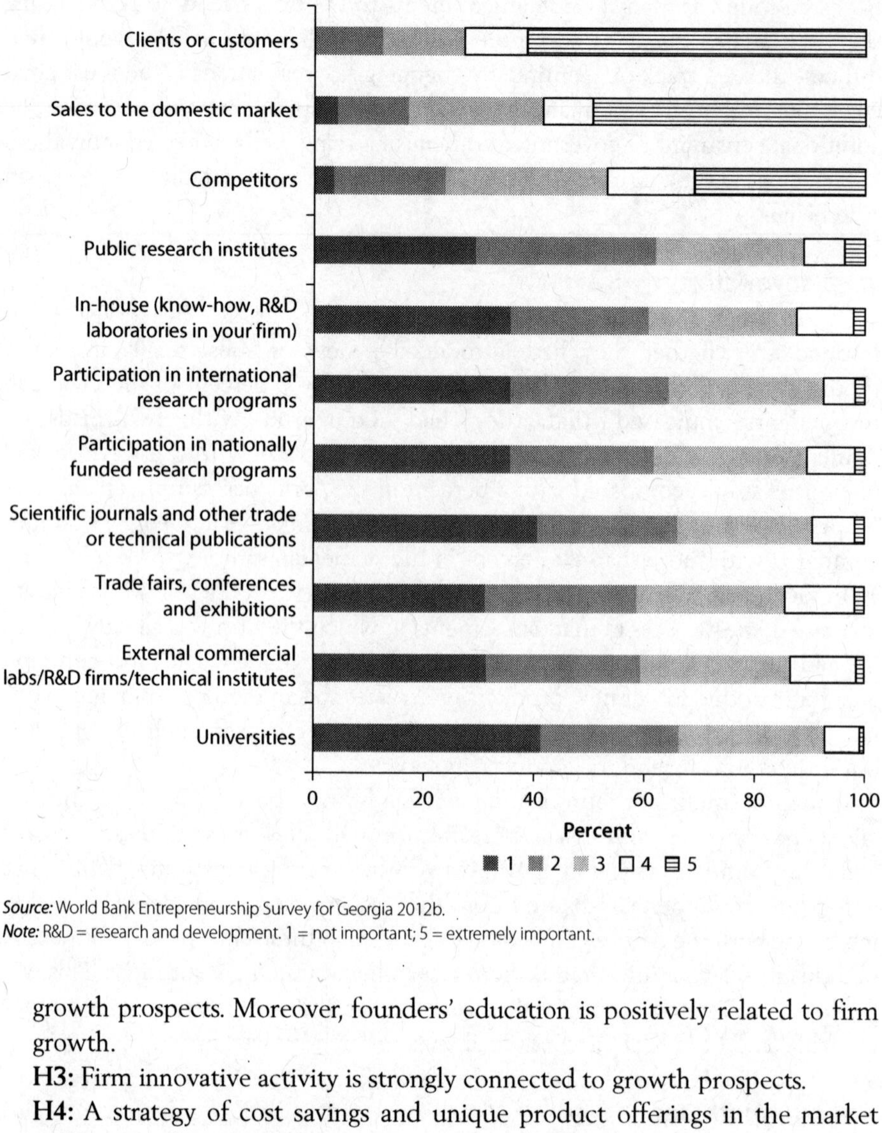

Source: World Bank Entrepreneurship Survey for Georgia 2012b.
Note: R&D = research and development. 1 = not important; 5 = extremely important.

growth prospects. Moreover, founders' education is positively related to firm growth.

H3: Firm innovative activity is strongly connected to growth prospects.

H4: A strategy of cost savings and unique product offerings in the market underwrites firm growth.

H5: An ability to access external capital is positively related to firm growth prospects.

Controls included market environment characteristics and growth trends of other companies in the same sector.

The results for Georgia are mixed (see table C.1). Only three variables besides the control were statistically significant: firm size, firm founders' industry experience, and ability to attract venture capital. All were positively related to firm growth rates. Fast-growing sectors were associated with fast-growing firms.

The results for the Armenian sample show that firm characteristics, entrepreneur characteristics, innovative activity, and firm strategy have significant explanatory power over firm sales growth. Younger firms with younger founders grew faster. Founders' prior industry experience was important for firm growth. The introduction of both innovative and unique products and services was positively associated with higher firm growth. A low-cost strategy was also associated with higher firm growth. Funding and market environment variables did not explain firm growth. Finally, the dynamism of the sector in which the company operates proved to be a significant explanatory factor.

A second model to explain the determinants of firm innovation used a probit regression (see box C.2 for the specifications).

The following hypotheses were tested:

H1: Younger, smaller firms innovate more.
H2: Firms in high-tech sectors and firms undertaking R&D innovate more.
H3: Founders' expertise at firm setup is an important indicator of innovation propensity. Founders' education background, especially in technical and engineering fields, is positively related to company innovativeness.
H4: Exposure to international markets is strongly connected to innovation propensity.
H5: Favorable outlook toward R&D and the formation of strategic partnerships with other organizations, including universities, research institutes, and private sector firms, are strong predictors of higher innovation propensity.
H6: Strategy to offer unique products and exploit opportunities in new market niches goes hand-in-hand with higher innovation propensity.

Regression results are shown in table C.2.

In Georgia only three variables besides the control were statistically significant: R&D intensity, founders' general management experience, and networking with research organizations. All were positively related to firm innovative propensity. There was a positive correlation between firm innovation and R&D activity being considered an important factor in creating and sustaining competitive advantage. Similarly, there was a positive correlation between innovative activity and when firm founders considered partnerships with research organizations such as universities an important factor in creating and sustaining competitive advantage. And firm innovation was higher in sectors with higher average rates of innovation.

In Azerbaijan firm age and size were significant variables. Younger firms and firms with more employees were positively correlated to firm innovative propensity. Further, strategic alliances with other companies and a strategy to offer unique products/services or exploit new market niches were also positively related. In Azerbaijan firm innovation was also higher in sectors with higher average rates of innovation.

In Armenia general management expertise of founders, international sales, perceived importance of R&D activity, and a strategy to offer unique products/services or exploit new market niches positively affected innovation propensity. International sales were positively associated with innovation propensity. There was a positive correlation between founders' perception of R&D being an important factor for competitive advantage and innovative activity in the firm. A strategy to offer unique products/services or exploit new market niches was naturally linked to higher innovation propensity. Finally, pressure from competitors in more innovative sectors promoted innovative propensity.

The next chapter looks at entrepreneurial activity in existing firms by analyzing the extent of innovation in the sample of surveyed firms in the World Bank Business Enterprise and Enterprise Performance Survey.

Notes

1. Details of data sources are described in appendix C.
2. This section is based on Atasoy and others (forthcoming). For details on the literature on and definition of latent entrepreneurship, see appendix A.
3. All the observations for the South Caucasus were analyzed as a pooled sample, rather than as separate country samples, to create a sufficiently large sample for analysis. Fixed country effects were incorporated into the analysis.
4. Chemical industry, manufacture of basic pharmaceutical products, manufacture of computer and other electronic equipment, manufacture of electrical equipment, and information and communication.

References

Atasoy, H., C. Sanchez-Paramo, E. R. Tiongson, and P. van der Zwan. Forthcoming. "Latent Entrepreneurship in the Europe and Central Asia (ECA) Region."

Gallup. 2011. World Poll Survey, 2011 edition. http://www.gallup.com.

Global Entrepreneurship Monitor. 2011. *Women's Report 2010*. London: Global Entrepreneurship Monitor.

World Bank. 2012a. *Entrepreneurship Database, 2012 edition*. Washington, DC.

———. 2012b. *Entrepreneurship Survey for Georgia*. Washington, DC: World Bank.

———. 2013. *World Development Indicators 2013*. Washington, DC: World Bank.

CHAPTER 4

Entrepreneurship and Innovation

Introduction

This chapter uses data from the World Bank's Enterprise Surveys to analyze entrepreneurial activity in existing firms as measured by their innovative activity. Four types of innovation activities are analyzed: introducing new products or services in the previous three years (product innovation), upgrading an existing product line or service in the previous three years (process innovation), investing in research and development, and licensing foreign technology.

In Armenia, Azerbaijan, and Georgia nearly 400 firms were surveyed, and they were roughly evenly distributed across manufacturing, retail, and services sectors. Almost half the samples were small firms, and a third were medium-size firms (see table D.1 for the size and industrial sector distribution of the samples from each country).

Innovation activities in the three South Caucasus countries are benchmarked against a group of 10 Europe and Central Asia (ECA) countries as well as all 25 ECA countries. The ECA-10 group includes eight members of the European Union (the Czech Republic, Estonia, Hungary, Latvia, Lithuania, Poland, the Slovak Republic, and Slovenia) and two large ECA countries (the Russian Federation and Turkey).

Process innovation is the most common type of innovation activity across the South Caucasus countries and other ECA countries. In every ECA country except Romania and Uzbekistan, at least half of firms reported conducting process innovation. In ECA 70 percent of firms conducted process innovation. Spending on research and development (R&D) and licensing foreign technology were seen in 20 percent of firms, half the proportion that engaged in product innovation. This is common in developing countries. Most innovation is through technology adoption and adaptation, usually described as non-R&D innovation.

South Caucasus countries had similar levels of process innovation; roughly three-quarters of firms upgraded an existing product line or service in the previous three years (figure 4.1). Product innovation was much less common than process innovation in the rest of ECA. Azerbaijan (41 percent) and Georgia (35 percent) had lower product innovation rates than the ECA-10 group

Figure 4.1 Innovation Rates by Country

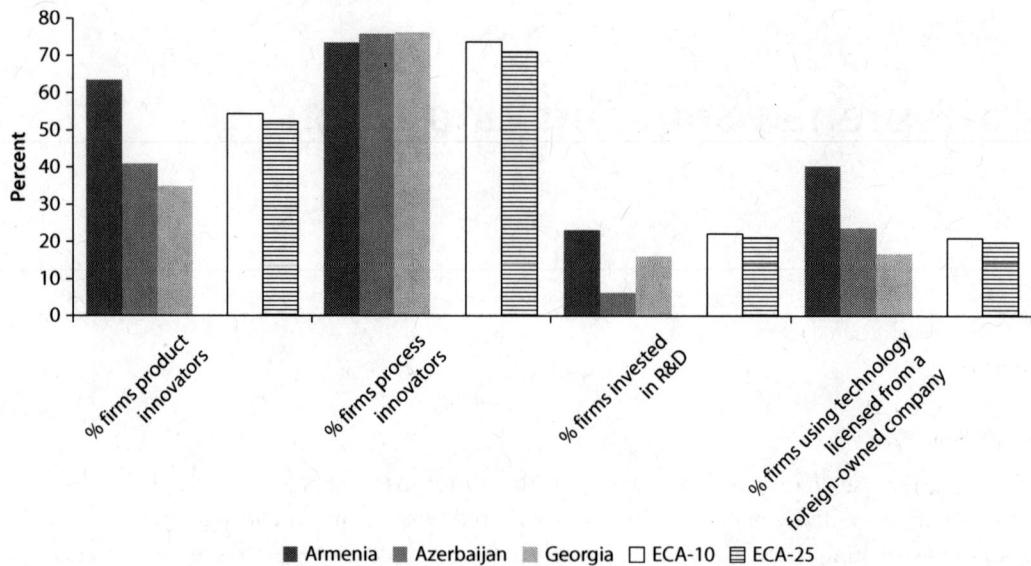

Source: World Bank Enterprise Surveys.
Note: ECA-10 countries are the Czech Republic, Estonia, Hungary, Latvia, Lithuania, Poland, the Russian Federation, the Slovak Republic, Slovenia, and Turkey. The ECA-25 group includes countries in the ECA-10 as well as Belarus, Bosnia and Herzegovina, Bulgaria, Kazakhstan, Kosovo, the Kyrgyz Republic, the former Yugoslav Republic of Macedonia, Moldova, Mongolia, Montenegro, Poland, Romania, Serbia, Tajikistan, Ukraine, and Uzbekistan. R&D = research and development.

(54 percent). They also invested less in R&D (6 percent in Azerbaijan and 16 percent in Georgia compared with 22 percent in ECA-10).

In the South Caucasus only Armenia had R&D spending rates comparable to those of the ECA-10 countries—23 percent in Armenia compared with 22 percent in the ECA-10. Armenian firms introduced more new product varieties and licensed more foreign technology than the average ECA-10 firm. This corroborates the evidence from the Entrepreneurship Survey as well as the case studies, in which Armenian firms undertook more innovative activity and spent more on R&D than their counterparts in Georgia and Azerbaijan.

Across all countries, large firms were consistently more likely than small firms to spend on R&D or to license technology from a foreign-owned company. In Georgia there was a gap in large product innovation between large firms (61 percent) and small firms (24 percent; figure 4.2). The disparity in R&D investment between large and small firms was also wide (57 percent compared with 7 percent).

Innovation and Investment Climate

Innovative firms are likely to differ from noninnovative firms in characteristics and activities. For example, in the three South Caucasus countries studied, innovative firms are much more likely than noninnovative firms to offer formal training.

Figure 4.2 Innovation Rates by Firm Size, Georgia

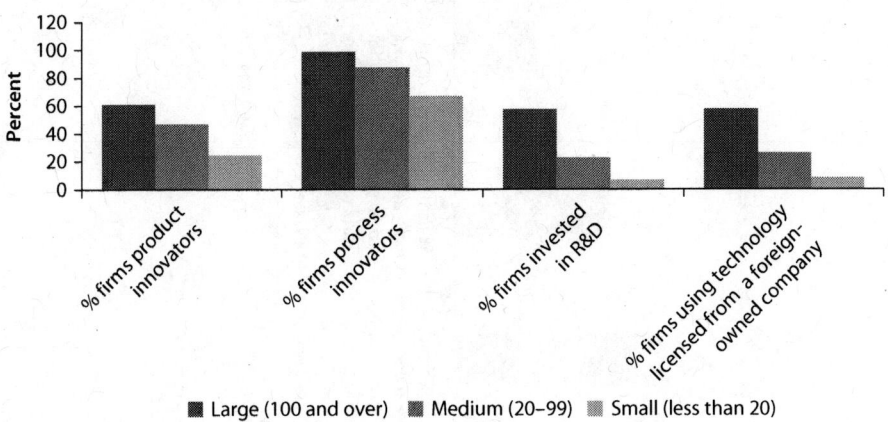

■ Large (100 and over) ■ Medium (20–99) ■ Small (less than 20)

Source: World Bank Enterprise Surveys.
Note: R&D = research and development.

Enterprise Surveys provide a wide range of corruption data from which several corruption indicators can be constructed. Only indicators that are statistically different between innovators (firms that participate in either product or process innovation) and noninnovators are presented in figure 4.3. In Armenia, Azerbaijan, and Georgia innovative firms experienced significantly more bribery and corruption than did noninnovative firms across a variety of measures.

In Georgia innovative firms were almost three times more likely to identify corruption as a major constraint to daily business operations than were noninnovative firms. In both Armenia and Azerbaijan four Enterprise Survey corruption indicators were statistically different between innovators and noninnovators. In Armenia Innovative firms were more likely to be expected to give informal gifts to obtain an operating license, "get things done," and get a construction permit. The incidence of graft,[1] which shows the percentage of business transactions that include bribes, was twice as high for innovative firms as for noninnovative firms. In Azerbaijan a larger percentage of innovative firms than noninnovative firms expected to have to give informal payments to obtain an operating license, electrical connection, or water connection. Moreover, the value of the bribe given to government officials to secure a government contract was much higher for innovative than noninnovative firms.

In Georgia innovative firms were also more likely to offer training than noninnovative firms. When the data are disaggregated by whether a firm is a process innovator, there is no difference in training offerings in the three South Caucasus countries. Innovative firms were significantly more likely to export than noninnovative firms in Georgia, Poland, Russia, and Turkey (figure 4.4). These results also hold when considering only product innovators or process innovators in isolation.

In Georgia innovative firms were significantly more likely to report political instability as a top obstacle to daily business operations than were noninnovative

Figure 4.3 Corruption Indicator Comparisons

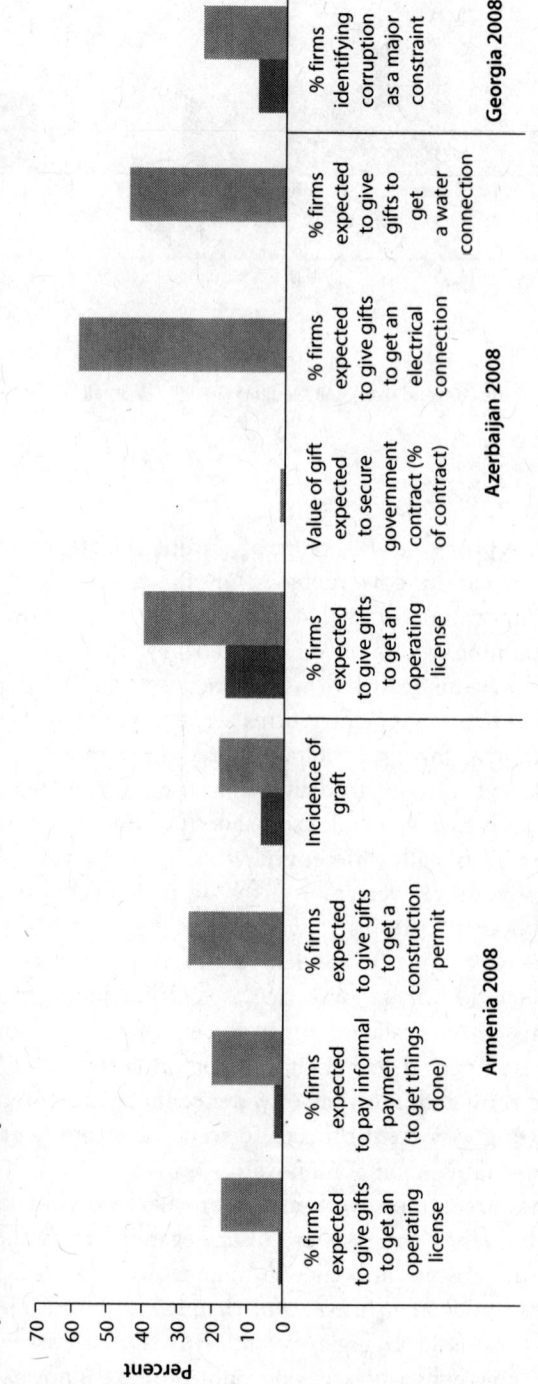

Source: World Bank Enterprise Surveys.

44

Figure 4.4 Innovative Activity by Exporting Status

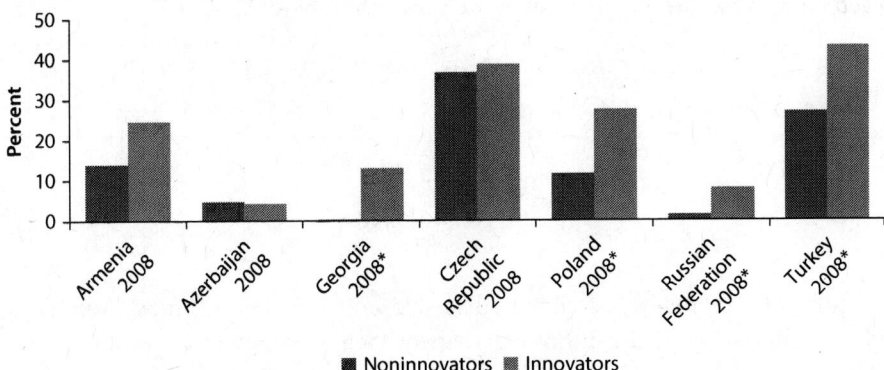

Source: World Bank Enterprise Surveys.
Note: A firm is considered an exporter if at least 10 percent of annual sales are derived from direct exports. A firm is considered an innovator if it participated in either product or process innovation.
*Statistically significant difference in the means at the 0.01 level.

Figure 4.5 Share of Firms Whose Top Obstacle Is Political Instability

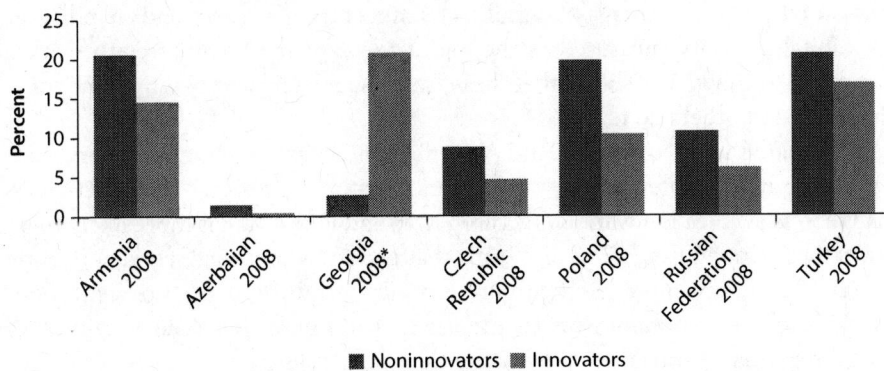

Source: World Bank Enterprise Surveys.
Note: A firm is considered an exporter if at least 10 percent of annual sales are derived from direct exports. A firm is considered an innovator if it participated in either product or process innovation.
*Statistically significant difference in the means at the 0.01 level.

firms (figure 4.5). Moreover, among the Southern Caucasus and the four comparator countries (the Czech Republic, Poland, Russia, and Turkey), Georgia is the only country where this difference is significant.

Who Are the Innovators?

The previous section showed that innovative and noninnovative firms differ across several characteristics. This section uses regression analysis to examine what firm characteristics are correlated with innovation activities. Probit regressions are estimated in which the dependent variable (Y_{jc}^{i}) is a dummy variable indicating whether firm j in country c conducted one of the four innovation activities (i) described above (equation 4.1). Regressions are run separately for each country, and estimation tables are shown in tables D.3–D.7.

$$Y_{jc}^{*i} = c + Z_{jc}\beta + \delta \text{Age}_{jc} + \varphi \text{Sector}_{jc} + \rho \text{Size}_{jc} + \varepsilon_{jc}^i \tag{4.1}$$

$$Y_{jc}^i = \begin{cases} 1 & \text{if } Y_{jc}^{*i} > 0 \\ 0 & \text{otherwise} \end{cases}$$

Empirical evidence has shown that size and age are the most important observable characteristics of firms that affect their activities. In the probit regression outlined above, age and size controls are included in the baseline specification. In addition, sector fixed effects are included to account for the differences in factors that affect innovation, such as the nature of market activity, competition level, technology use, and demand. Explanatory variables of interest (Z) are included in the regression separately, one at a time. The set of key explanatory variables of interest includes variables for whether a firm is an exporter, has foreign ownership,[2] and offers formal training; an indicator for skill intensity, measured as the percentage of unskilled manufacturing workers; and an indicator of capital intensity, measured as the log of the capital expenditures to worker ratio. Existing evidence shows that these factors can be related to why some firms innovate and others do not.

Compared with Azerbaijan and Armenia, innovation activities in Georgia are more likely to differ across firm characteristics and other firm activities. In Georgia average innovation rates are lower, and innovation is more likely to be an activity among large firms and firms that export. Moreover, Georgian exporters are 36 percent more likely to introduce new products, and 19 percent more likely to be process innovators (see tables D.3 and D.4). Yet trade activity does not differentiate innovation activity in other ECA countries.[3]

In Georgia whether a firm offers formal training is also closely tied to whether it spends on R&D (see table D.5). The magnitude of this relationship is higher than in Armenia or Azerbaijan and the selected comparator countries. In Georgia firms that offer formal training are also 62 percent more likely to spend on R&D. Russian firms that offer formal training are 32 percent more likely to spend on R&D, and Turkish firms are 16 percent more likely to.

While it may seem certain that firms that have foreign ownership are more likely to license foreign-owned technology, this relationship is only significant in Georgia (see table D.6). Georgian firms that have at least 10 percent foreign ownership are 41 percent more likely to license foreign-owned technology. This may suggest that foreign ownership in Georgia is an important source of knowledge and technology diffusion.

A major concern with country-specific regression analysis is the small sample size. To alleviate this problem, the same probit model is estimated with the samples of the three South Caucasus countries pooled together. Another motivation for this exercise is to see how the overall performances of Southern Caucasus countries differ from more developed ECA economies. To control for country differences, country dummy variables are included (equation 4.2).

$$Y_{jc}^{*i} = c + Z_{jc}\beta + \delta \text{Age}_{jc} + \varphi \text{Sector}_{jc} + \rho \text{Size}_{jc} + \theta \text{country}_{jc} + \varepsilon_{jc}^{i} \qquad (4.2)$$

$$Y_{jc}^{i} = \begin{cases} 1 & \text{if } Y_{jc}^{*i} > 0 \\ 0 & \text{otherwise} \end{cases}$$

Regression results using the pooled sample of three countries show that firm size is positively correlated with conducting all four innovation activities (see table D.7).

The most significant correlates of product innovation in the region were exporting, offering formal training, and the capital expenditure to worker ratio. Firms that export were 21 percent more likely to be product innovators, firms that offer formal training were 31 percent more likely, and there is a significant positive relationship between capital expenditure to worker ratio and product innovation.

The only significant correlate of process innovation was the proportion of unskilled manufacturing workers in a firm, and the magnitude of the correlation was very small. Firms that offer training were 0.3 percent more likely to be process innovators. Training is an integral part of firm strategy, as evidenced by the firms interviewed for the case studies, since firms need to equip staff with the required skills to keep their competitive advantage.

Foreign ownership predicts the licensing of technology from a foreign-owned company but not of any other type of innovation activity. Foreign-owned firms are 22 percent more likely to license foreign technology.

Innovation and Firm Performance

The annual real sales growth of innovative firms in Armenia and Georgia was twice as high as in comparator countries. In Armenia noninnovating firms also had twice as much growth as the respective group in the comparator countries.[4] The annual sales growth of innovative firms was significantly higher than that of noninnovative firms in both Georgia and Azerbaijan (figure 4.6). In both countries the revenues of noninnovative firms decreased; in Georgia the decrease was more than 20 percent.

As with sales growth, employment growth rates were significantly higher for innovative firms in Armenia and Georgia than for firms in the comparator countries (figure 4.7). In all countries in the figure, innovative firms had higher employment growth, yet the difference was significant only in Georgia and the Czech Republic. The high performance of innovative firms in Armenia and Georgia persisted in labor productivity growth, which is measured as total sales

Figure 4.6 Average Annual Sales Growth

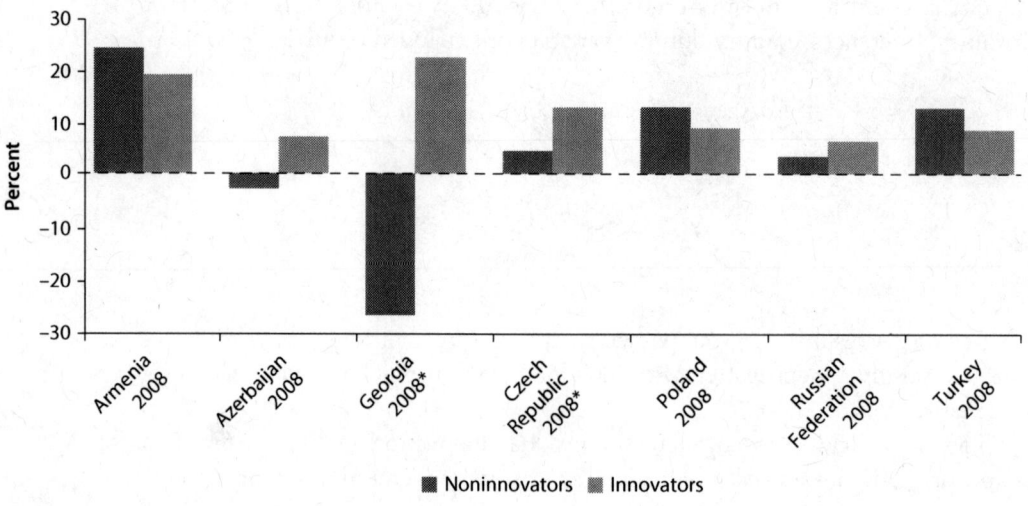

Source: World Bank Enterprise Surveys.
Note: A firm is considered to be an innovator if it participated in either product or process innovation.
*Statistically significant difference in the means at the 0.01 level.

Figure 4.7 Average Annual Employment Growth

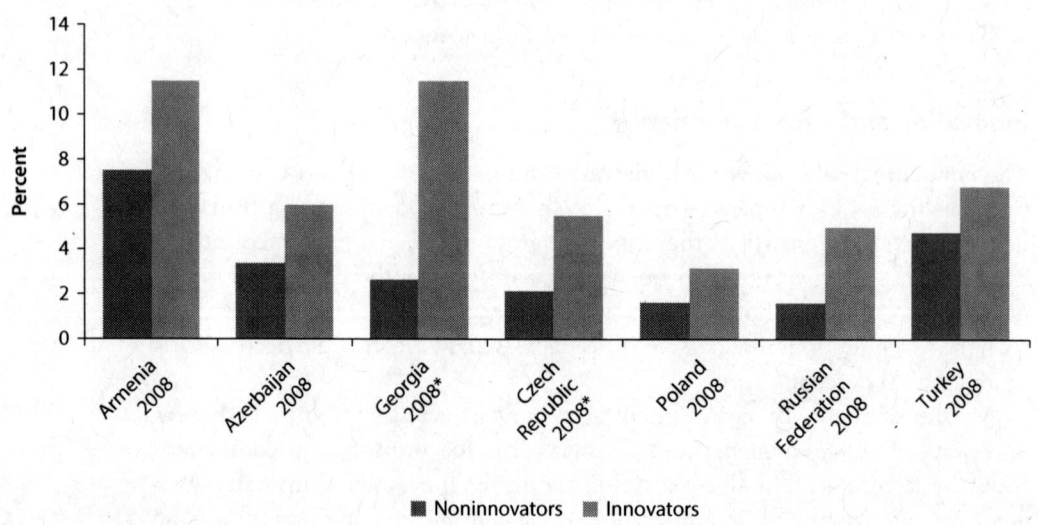

Source: World Bank Enterprise Surveys.
Note: A firm is considered to be an innovator if it participated in either product or process innovation.
*Statistically significant difference in the means at the 0.01 level.

Figure 4.8 Average Annual Labor Productivity Growth

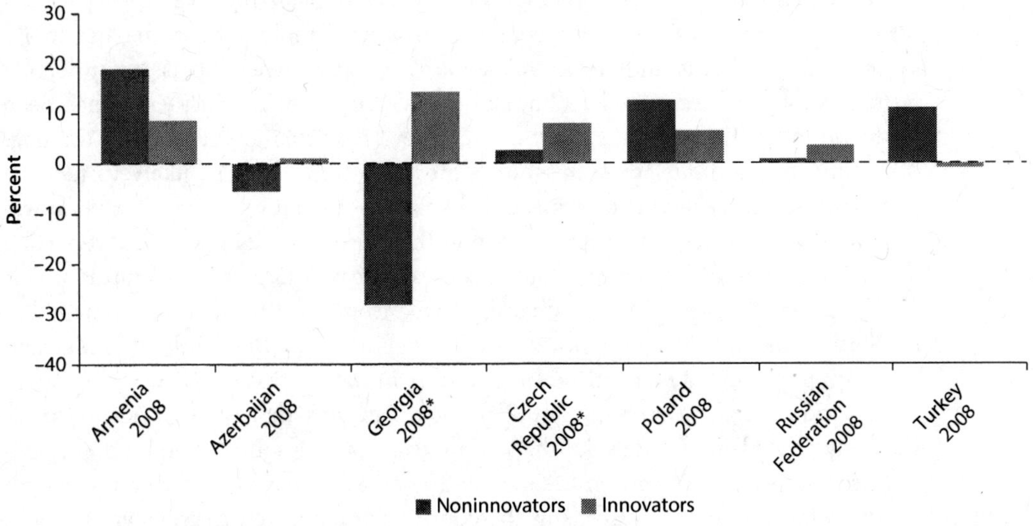

Source: World Bank Enterprise Surveys.
Note: A firm is considered to be an innovator if it participated in either product or process innovation.
*Statistically significant difference in the means at the 0.01 level.

per number of workers (figure 4.8). The closest follower of Armenia and Georgia in the comparator country group was the Czech Republic. In Armenia, Poland, and Turkey innovative firms had lower productivity growth than noninnovative firms.

The link between innovation and firm performance is a key relationship of interest. A series of ordinary least squares regressions were estimated to examine this relationship more closely (equation 4.3). Regressions were estimated for each country separately. Three measures of firm performance (G_{jc}) were considered: annual real sales growth, annual employment growth, and annual real labor productivity growth. The main variable of interest in the regressions is a dummy variable set to 1 if the firm has engaged in an innovation activity (Innovation$_{jc}$). In addition, there are controls for size, age, and the sector of the firm.

$$G_{jc} = c + \gamma \, \text{Innovation}_{jc} + Z_{jc}\,\beta + \delta \text{Age}_{jc} + \varphi \, \text{Sector}_{jc} + \rho \, \text{Size}_{jc} + \varepsilon_{jc} \quad (4.3)[5]$$

Product innovation and annual employment growth were significantly positively related in all three Southern Caucasus countries (see table D.8). Product innovation predicted that employment growth would be about 6.6 percent higher for Armenian firms, 3.5 percent higher for Azerbaijani firms, and 9 percent higher for Georgian firms. As for sales growth, only firms in Georgia have higher performance relative to other countries when conducting innovation. Firms that conducted product or process innovation, or spent on R&D, experienced sales growth that was 10–12 percent higher than firms that did not (see table D.9).

The analysis in this chapter shows that significant differences exist between firms that innovate and firms that do not in Georgia. While average innovation rates are lower in Georgia in general, innovation is more likely to be an activity among large firms and firms that export. Foreign ownership is an important source of knowledge and technology transfer in Georgia. Further, as has been found in the Entrepreneurship Survey, innovative firms spend more on training.

In Georgia, innovative firms are almost three times more likely to identify corruption as a major constraint to daily business operations than are noninnovative firms. This could reflect the fact that these firms are doing well and reporting higher growth and revenue, which makes them easier targets for corruption. This is in line with some of the feedback received from firms in the Entrepreneurship Survey that would rather not grow in order to remain beneath the radar and continue to operate unnoticed by government authorities.

Product innovation and annual employment growth were significantly positively related in all three Southern Caucasus countries. Both sales and employment in innovative firms in Georgia had significantly faster growth rates than in the respective group of firms in the comparator countries. Regression estimates also suggest that in Georgia sales growth is higher in innovative firms than in noninnovative firms. These results further strengthen the link between innovation and firm growth as well as the role of the government in fostering an environment conducive to innovative activity among existing firms and new high-growth entrepreneurialism.

Notes

1. This indicator was the percentage of firms experiencing at least one bribe payment request across six public transactions dealing with utilities access, permits, licenses, and taxes.

2. A foreign-owned firm is defined as a firm with at least 10 percent ownership by a foreign individual or company.

3. When compared to Armenia, Azerbaijan, the Czech Republic, Poland, Russia, or Turkey.

4. The Czech Republic, Poland, Russia, and Turkey.

5. In another exercise the contribution of innovation to firm growth was compared in Southern Caucasus countries and ECA-10 countries. The equation is similar to equation 4.2 but with the addition of an interaction term between dummy variables for innovation activity i and country c. The coefficient is the parameter of interest. A significantly positive coefficient signals that an innovation activity i contributes to higher growth when conducted by firms in country c. There were no significant estimates of the coefficient in this exercise.

Reference

World Bank Enterprise Surveys database. http://www.enterprisesurveys.org.

CHAPTER 5

How Can Government Policies Stimulate Entrepreneurship?

Introduction

Governments can support entrepreneurial activities in a variety of ways. At the most basic level, effective government policies can create an institutional base that establishes openness to trade, improves the business environment for domestic and foreign investment, establishes effective intellectual property rights regimes, and enhances knowledge flows and learning. Beyond those general policies, many governments have also intervened at the industry and firm levels to address market failures.

While several factors in Georgia contribute to a positive business environment for small and medium enterprises (SMEs), they are insufficient for rapid business growth or fostering entrepreneurship. Financial systems are not conducive to business development. Companies cite high interest rates and risk-averse lending policies (requiring high levels of collateral) as substantial hindrances to expansion. In addition, risk capital is in short supply. Few entrepreneurs reported receiving funding from the domestic financial system; most relied on their own resources to support the development of their business.

In Georgia the State Commission for Regional Development is responsible for innovation policy schemes to support new technologies and entrepreneurship. The commission is supported by a task force for regional development and seven working groups. The working group on innovation, new technologies, and entrepreneurship brings together experts and policymakers and makes recommendations for innovation policy. Despite these institutions, Georgia does not have a specific SME policy or an innovation strategy. SME support is loosely integrated into the State Strategy for Regional Development of Georgia for 2010–17, which incorporates support for developing innovation, new technologies, and entrepreneurship as one of its objectives. But it does not have an implementation plan with clear objectives or targets.

Minimal infrastructure is in place to respond to business needs. The Georgian Chamber of Commerce and Industry, the Business Association of Georgia, the Employers' Association of Georgia, the International Chamber of Commerce, and the Tax Ombudsman's Office all provide information and business services to help Georgian enterprises. But there is poor coordination among these institutions, leading to duplication as well as inefficiency of services.

No specific instruments are in place that foster entrepreneurial or innovative activity. And lack of both technical and managerial skills was cited more often than not as a constraint faced by high-growth firms, which relied heavily on foreign expertise and extensive on-the-job training due to the lack of industry-relevant skills available in the market.

Governments play an important role in providing high-quality framework conditions by removing bottlenecks in the general business environment that impede able entrepreneurs with good ideas from starting a new venture and creating jobs. These conditions include well functioning institutions, competitive markets for inputs and outputs, a predictable system of taxation, and bankruptcy legislation that facilitates resource reallocation while protecting creditors (Nolan 2003). The government thus facilitates a conducive business environment that allows failure and company exit as a necessary part of entrepreneurial learning, provides company incentives that favor entrepreneurs with good ideas, introduces instruments that enable entrepreneurs to access capital for startups, and ensures flexible labor market policies that enable firms to expand by attracting the best talents from outside the firm or the country.

Beginning in 2006, the government implemented reforms in a range of areas to support a liberal business environment. Most noticeably, the government has reduced bureaucracy, improved tax policies, fought corruption, and liberalized labor regulations. Reforms in tax law, customs law, employment law, and legislation governing licensing have made it much easier to start and run a business. But avenues still exist for these to be improved to further facilitate entrepreneurial activity.

Increasing Access to Finance

Little risk capital is available to startups, and bank borrowing is expensive. Nearly all the surveyed firms had been established with personal savings, funds borrowed from friends and families, and in some cases concessional loans financed by the European Bank for Reconstruction and Development. Only after establishing themselves as creditworthy did enterprises turn to banks to borrow funds to expand their ventures. They also agreed on needing to have other sources of finances and needing to develop the financial infrastructure to support varied support instruments for new ventures.

The banking sector is dominated by a few large banks. Of the 19 banks operating in Georgia, the top 5 control close to 80 percent of assets. Only 21 percent of domestic credit to the private sector goes to SMEs, as the large banks focus primarily on financing large enterprises (OECD 2012). Procredit Bank is one of the only lenders targeting SMEs, but it lends to very small firms that are not too risky and could potentially be high-growth SMEs.

During the early stages of new innovative companies, which usually have few or no sources of revenue and require large initial capital investments to develop their products, loan payments have a high opportunity cost. For this reason, loans are usually most appropriate for companies that already have steady revenue streams. For startups that are in their nascent stages and focused on developing their first products, equity investments tend to be a better option.

The government can establish favorable financing programs for SMEs by developing early-stage risk capital. The role of early-stage risk capital is highly relevant for innovative startups and SMEs. Startups lack access to adequate capital due to the high-risk nature of investments and the lack of access to bank credit due to their insufficient collateral. Innovative SMEs thus rely on investors who provide risk capital, generally in return for a share of the company. Several countries have undertaken efforts toward creating and strengthening the venture capital industry. Brazil and Chile are pioneers in this field, although through different strategies and approaches (see box 5.1; Kantis and Federico 2011).[1]

Some countries also use loan guarantee schemes that address market imperfections in providing debt finance for small firms. These schemes help ensure that good projects are not precluded from access to finance due to lack of collateral. A premium interest rate may be charged on the loan, but in the event of default, the government covers some of the loss.

In designing new financial policy instruments to foster entrepreneurship and innovation, care should be taken in both designing and managing these instruments to prevent capture or corruption and to promote efficiency. The following elements are important:

- Clearly established goals and objectives at the outset.
- Constant monitoring and evaluation of performance as against goals and objectives.
- Monitoring and evaluation performed externally to the administration and management of the instruments.
- Adjudication to approve applications, conducted by an independent panel consisting of external peer reviewers.
- An independent panel with significant private sector and export expertise.
- Adjudication based on pre-established, clear, and transparent criteria.

Simplifying Tax Administration

While overall tax legislation is good for firms, its enforcement was reported to be uncertain occasionally. Individuals want more standardization and consistency in its applications. A breakdown of the results of the World Bank Enterprise Survey of 2008 revealed important differences in the perceived constraints between smaller and larger Georgian businesses. Since the adoption of the new tax code in 2005, there was a single tax treatment for all taxpayers, with same rates and compliance requirements for micro, small, medium, and large taxpayers. Thus, while the share of large and medium businesses that rated tax administration as

Box 5.1 Case Study: Brazil—INOVAR

Entrepreneurship has been a core theme in the economic success of Brazil, which now has the second largest economy in the Western Hemisphere and the sixth largest in the world. Over the past 20 years Brazil has undergone impressive development. SMEs have been integral in this development, responsible for 96 percent of jobs and 98 percent of companies. The Brazilian government has several policy support measures that range from concessional loans to technical assistance, mentoring, and incubation services.

One of the major challenges in Brazil, as in many developing countries, is unleashing private capital for investment in innovative business models. With this goal in mind, Brazil established INOVAR to develop capacity for a venture capital environment. INOVAR was founded in 2000 by the Brazilian Agency for Innovation with assistance from the Inter-American Development Bank's Multilateral Investment Fund. The goal of the program is to catalyze a private equity market in Brazil by using a strategy with three components: a Technology Investment Facility, an INOVAR Forum, and venture capital training programs.

The Technology Investment Facility is a structured program that trains potential investors to analyze and assess the value of venture capital funds. A major goal of the program at its outset was to convince pension fund managers in Brazil to invest in domestic venture capital opportunities. In the early 2000s Brazil had 366 pension funds that were allowed to invest up to 20 percent of their capital in private equity firms, but due to a lack of familiarity with the sector, they were unwilling to do so (Leamon and Lerner 2012). The Technology Investment Facility addresses this barrier by training potential investors to understand different aspects of venture capital funds and the risks they face. Through the program, participants communicate with fund operators about their analysis, providing them with valuable feedback and insight into how they could better satisfy the demands of investors. In doing so INOVAR is facilitating partnerships between investors and fund owners, and is training participants in the management, design, and assessment of venture capital funds.

The second component of INOVAR's strategy is its Venture Forums program, which trains entrepreneurs and provides a platform for matching investors with one another. The program selects promising entrepreneurs to appear before market professionals and other experts to pitch their businesses and possibly receive business coaching. The coaching focuses on fundraising, developing business plans, and training in high-growth strategies. Following the coaching sessions, entrepreneurs are then given the opportunity to meet with potential investors and perhaps negotiate for an investment or acquisition. The program targets businesses at various stages of development, from early-stage companies not yet marketing products at one end of the spectrum, through ones where managers are preparing to take their firms public. To complement its training and mentoring efforts for entrepreneurs and established investors, INOVAR also engages in venture capital training as the third component of its strategy. This training is designed to increase the pool of venture capitalists in the country and expose participants to international best practices.

INOVAR's efforts have led to investments of more than $1 billion of private equity and venture capital (Leamon and Lerner 2012). The initiative has been credited with greatly

box continues next page

Box 5.1 Case Study: Brazil—INOVAR *(continued)*

increasing the participation of pension funds in the venture capital sector and has improved the general environment for acquiring venture capital in the country. Only one pension fund participated in the Technology Investment Facility at its outset; the program grew to include 11 pension funds by the end of 2011, including the top five in the country. The INOVAR model has been followed by other countries in the region, including Chile, Colombia, and Mexico.

---

a major obstacle from 2005 to 2008 decreased (large by 22 percent and medium by 9 percent), the share of small businesses complaining about the same issue in the same period *increased* by 9 percent—from 11 percent to 20 percent.

The Ministry of Economy and Sustainable Development established the Business Activity Regulatory Impact Division to analyze the impact of laws and regulations on the business environment. From 2006 to 2010, approximately 21,000 legal acts were reviewed through a rigorous legislative guillotine process, and more than half—12,000—were abolished (OECD 2012). Legislative streamlining was conducted in such areas as public and administrative services, public procurement, public finance, company/entrepreneurial legislation, and tax and customs systems. The tax system was dramatically simplified, with a reduction in the number of taxes from 22 to 6 by 2008. Moreover, the 2005 tax code simplified the business registration and tax payment process and reduced the number of documents required for registration. Nevertheless, the changes to the tax code have been numerous over the last year, making them difficult in particular for SMEs to keep track of. Analyses by GeoWel Research show that in 2011, there were 285 changes to the tax code and another 135 through June 2012.

Greater transparency and certainty must be ensured in the tax system. The government should announce any changes to the tax code at least six months before their implementation to make it easier for firms to follow them.

Facilitating Learning from Exporting and Fostering Backward Links through Foreign Direct Investment Growth

The analyses in chapters 3 and 4 showed that openness to trade is an important source of knowledge transfer and an important motivation for firms to undertake entrepreneurial activities that increase market share, productivity, and growth. Such a phenomenon, sometimes referred to as "learning from exporting," often takes place when exporting firms are under pressure to meet quality standards, including safety and environmental regulations, established by their customers or the regulatory authorities of destination countries. Such pressures can either strengthen incentives for exporting firms to upgrade their technology or hinder other firms that lack the requisites for exporting to more sophisticated markets.

The new government of Georgia has recommitted to expanding exports into new products and markets as a key component of the economy's continued growth. The European Union has been identified as a main target for trade diversification and expansion. Between 2005 and 2011 the share of exports going to the European Union dropped from 25 percent to 19 percent. At the same time, the share going to Turkey and the Commonwealth of Independent State countries (excluding the Russian Federation) increased (World Bank 2012). In an effort to reverse this, the government set as one of its medium-term priorities increasing competitiveness by maintaining a free market environment with openness to international trade and establishing a deep and comprehensive free trade agreement with the European Union (World Bank 2011).

The Georgian government has also been developing strong trade partnerships through membership in the World Trade Organization, the Council of Europe, and the European Neighborhood Program. Georgia has Generalized System of Preference status with Canada, Japan, Norway, Switzerland, and the United States and Generalized System of Preference Plus status with the European Union and Turkey. Entry into these partnerships has supported harmonization to international standards and increased access to important markets such as the European Union.

Authorities are encouraging the diversification of exported goods to processed goods instead of raw materials, which previously accounted for the bulk of exports. A continued challenge in this effort is supporting the production of goods suitable for Western export markets, which will require improving product quality and consistency. To facilitate exports, the Georgian National Investment Agency's role was expanded to provide information for potential exporters on export procedures, foreign market requirements, trade regimes, and legislation. However, the agency has a severely constrained budget and capacity, which limits its scope of support.

While competition pressure helps provide needed incentives, insufficient capacity is often the binding constraint that prevents firms from learning more from exporting. Inability to adhere to minimum global standards, in particular, can be a major obstacle for firms to enter new export markets. Given the government's emphasis on export-led growth to help diversify the economy, it could focus on three priority areas:

- Introducing instruments of financial assistance to defray a portion of the cost that firms incur to acquire the requisite capacity. The Georgian National Investment Agency has been playing that role in Georgia by helping SMEs access international trade fairs to showcase their products. But the government provides no incentives to undertake research and development (R&D) or invest in new technologies. A matching grants program to support worker training and the purchase of consultancy services (including those required for quality certifications to adhere to global standards) should be considered. Firms would benefit from not having to bear the entire cost of the investment, and since they would match the portion paid for by the government, the program would attract genuinely committed firms. In Singapore, for example, the new Market Readiness Assistance Grant encourages more SMEs to expand their business overseas. Through this measure, Singapore-incorporated firms seeking overseas expansion can tap preapproved industry consultants in areas such as market assessment, market entry, business restructuring through internationalization, and the like.

- Providing basic infrastructure to enable firms to adhere to international standards. This is especially important for Georgia, where agroprocessing is a key priority sector for the economy. The government should invest in building accredited control laboratories that support firms in the agroprocessing industry, where adhering to global standards is a prerequisite for survival.

- Formulating policies to promote technology transfer to the domestic economy from foreign direct investment. For example, in 2003 the Chinese government and Microsoft signed a deal to use Windows as the preferred desktop operating system for government offices. In return Microsoft was required to reveal its Windows source codes to allay the government's security fears, to cooperate with the country's largest software development and integration firm to co-develop products based on Microsoft's software platforms, and to train 200 software developers and 120 architects within one year. Rather than simply allowing Microsoft to wire up the government's operations, the contract was clearly designed to promote technology diffusion (Kuriakose, Goldberg, and Zhang 2011).

A recent announcement by the Ministry of Economy and Sustainable Development stressed the importance of supporting foreign investment in Georgia, and a concerted effort is being made to actively engage existing investors and reach out to new investors. The ministry set up the Cooperation Council of Investors to actively work with the investor community and develop a special requirement list based on their feedback. The list is being used to prioritize infrastructure needs for new investors seeking to invest in Georgia. Since foreign direct investment can be an important source of know-how and technology transfer, special attention should be paid to incentives that encourage foreign firms to engage in transferring technology and skills to the domestic economy in Georgia.

This initiative could be further strengthened by the government formulating policies to promote backward links between foreign firms and the domestic economy, including acting as a facilitator and gathering information on possible opportunities for links,[2] assisting in identifying partners (and arrangements) by matching suppliers' capabilities and buyers' needs (legal assistance, fairs, missions, conferences and exhibitions, and so forth), and providing economic incentives in the form of tax exemptions and subsidies to promote training and technology transfer from buyer firms to local supplier firms.[3]

Developing Skills

Stakeholders repeatedly cited inadequate skills as a key hindrance to developing local industry. While the majority of the population has higher education, their skills are not aligned with industry needs, thus indicating a skills mismatch. In particular, both technical and management skills are lacking. This reflects the course curriculum's strong focus on theory, containing little practical education and almost fully removed from the market.

Despite various education reforms, a skills gap remains between the skills of Georgia's labor force and the needs of the enterprise sector. To improve the skills base and facilitate better alignment of labor force skills with the enterprise sector, education targets for the country include increased training in natural science disciplines. A technology university in Batumi is being established to develop a scientific training center that will focus on engineering, information technology, and agriculture and emphasize commercialization of scientific findings. *Medium- to long-term policies need to reorient the higher education system to produce more industry-relevant skills.*

Firms in Georgia could also benefit from training and mentoring graduates straight out of school. One measure for doing that is Singapore's SME Talent Program, which allows SMEs to sponsor study awards to qualified students of the institutes of technical education and polytechnics, followed by a job offer upon graduation. By attracting and nurturing talent, the program helps SMEs build a strong labor core.

In addition, more emphasis is needed on industry-relevant vocational training and education courses that cater to the technical needs of the various priority sectors identified by the government. In this process, a feedback mechanism between firms and the government is necessary, with feedback being provided to the design and development of new courses that respond to the skills needs of industry.

Another important area is the provision of adequate managerial and marketing competencies, as the analysis showed that many founders had these skills, which possibly set them apart and provided them with the requisite skills to start their entrepreneurial activity. Lack of managerial capital is an important constraint to firm growth (Bloom and Van Reenen 2010).[4] Support for existing firms to develop managerial and marketing competencies by subsidizing costs or direct procuring business development supply services and advisory services is common in developed economies. Vouchers, which allow firms to freely choose service providers, are used in several countries (for example, in Chile).

A way to provide business development supply services is through business incubators that supply entrepreneurs with the expertise, funding, networks, and tools they need to make their ventures successful (Etzkowitz and others 2005; Rothaermel 2002). In addition to physical space and shared infrastructure, incubators provide important soft skills, including professional consulting for business planning and strategy, project preparation, financial and legal assistance, and intermediation services, notably funding or linking to capital sources and integration to technology and business networks, among others. For example, the Republic of Korea's Institute of Startup and Entrepreneurship Development develops requisite skills by providing a range of support services that address various aspects of entrepreneurial development (see box 5.2).

Another important source of knowledge and skills transfer is access to networks of successful entrepreneurs who mentor other entrepreneurs venturing into startups. This could be done by tapping into the Georgian diaspora as well, thereby providing local entrepreneurs with global insights.

Box 5.2 Case Study: The Republic of Korea—Korea Institute of Startup and Entrepreneurship Development

Korea has a reputation for having one of the world's best education systems and a very welcoming business atmosphere (the World Bank ranks the country eighth in ease of doing business). With these advantages, Korea should be teeming with aspiring entrepreneurs. Nonetheless, cultural barriers such as an aversion to risk and failure have kept many would-be entrepreneurs from reaching their full potential. But over the past decade the country has bolstered support for startup enterprises and implemented several programs that foster an entrepreneurial spirit, changing the attitude toward entrepreneurship.

In 2008 Korea began implementing a series of policy packages known as the Start-up Korea Initiatives. These policies foster entrepreneurship with support structured around three themes: developing startup resources, enhancing startup capacity, and leveraging successful incubation. Leading this effort is the Korea Institute of Startup and Entrepreneurship Development, a public institute under the country's Small and Medium Business Administration. The institute was founded in 2000 as a nonprofit business incubation association but was designated by the government as the organization exclusively in charge of SME startup promotion in 2006, and it officially became a public entity in 2010. The institute is now the primary implementation agency for the Small and Medium Business Administration's startup initiatives.

The first theme of support involves developing the requisite skills and resources to set a backdrop for successful startup creation. The institute implemented five programs addressing various aspects of development:

- A program to support commercialization of creative ideas through content production, registration, and intellectual property protection.
- A program to cultivate entrepreneurs by providing them with financing for business preparation and access to resources at universities and research centers.
- A program to foster the spread of knowledge and know-how by linking successful ventures with fledgling startups to act as mentors and technology consultants.
- A program to encourage technology-oriented startups by providing access to patents held by universities and research organizations.
- A program to organize a variety of events to generate an entrepreneurial spirit among students.

---

box continues next page

Box 5.2 Case Study: The Republic of Korea—Korea Institute of Startup and Entrepreneurship Development (continued)

The second type of support measure is enhancing the capacity of potential entrepreneurs through a variety of education programs, clubs, and competitions. The Youth BizCool program grooms entrepreneurs at a young age by sponsoring clubs, activities, and education materials targeted to students from primary school through high school. University startup support programs continue building skills, with support for activities such as clubs and overseas startup training. Potential entrepreneurs who are not students can also participate in an education program for the general public, which offers mentoring and consulting on weekends. Other efforts also help build capacity in this phase, such as the Korea National Startup Competition League, which holds annual competitions. Successful teams in this competition earn prize money and cost compensation for their pilot products.

The third theme of support enhances the potential for businesses to succeed in the country's network of business incubators. At the end of 2010 Korea had 274 business incubators nationwide, which housed about 4,000 enterprises (KISED 2011). To improve the effectiveness of these incubators, the institute implemented a program to train and certify specialized business incubator managers. It offers the enterprises at these incubators support for marketing at home and abroad and provides commercialization support in the form of design and development assistance to promising businesses. The institute markets businesses that successfully commercialize products in newspapers, subway train ads, and e-books. Along with the startup support mechanisms discussed above, the institute supports Korean entrepreneurs through global outreach and cooperation with international partners to facilitate information exchange. So far, the country's efforts to support business creation appear to be paying off. Since 2008 the number of new business ventures and incorporations in Korea has steadily grown despite the global economic downturn.

Source: KISED n.d.

Increasing Industry-Research Collaboration and In-Firm R&D

An economy needs both researchers and entrepreneurs to be successful. Universities and industry are linked by the two groups, and the two groups require each other to be successful. But how is the relationship used to the best advantage? In several ways. The university could ask industry what appeared to be the most promising areas for product innovation and invention, or industries could ask what current research had the most commercial applications. Each must see the value of the relationship for any approach to be successful.

In Georgia, R&D is limited, even among high-growth firms, and there is virtually no industry-research collaboration. *Synergies must be built between these two communities in the priority areas identified by the government.* Examples of successful programs in other countries include India's Sponsored Research and Development program (SPREAD)—an early-stage technology development program that has been directed exclusively at private enterprises, with an explicit requirement for collaboration with public research institutes—which has been independently evaluated as successful.

Finland, Ireland, and Singapore provide important lessons. Yusuf and Nabeshima (2011) cite these three countries at the very outset, seeing in their strategies a vital role for university-industry links that led to a circulation of knowledge and of researchers. The universities were viewed as a source of entrepreneurship to help transfer innovation to the business sector. In Finland the Nokia Corporation took the lead in conjunction with the National Board of Education, the Ministry of Education, and the Future Committee of the Parliament in persuading the Academy of Finland to accelerate the initiative to become a knowledge society by mobilizing universities and public research entities. The role that the Finnish Funding Agency for Technology and Innovation had in Finland's transformation into a knowledge economy has been widely acknowledged. Established by the government in 1983, the agency has a broad mandate that includes identifying areas for technological advance and coordinating the working of the innovation system with the help of catalytic funding of R&D, all the while working closely with government agencies, universities, firms, and private financiers.

Technology transfer institutions are particularly important for firms in the process of catching up. Technology-bridging organizations can facilitate knowledge transfer from research institutions to SMEs through collaborative research and technology programs and through staff exchanges and secondments (placing researchers and engineers in firms). Yet to effectively absorb external knowledge and appropriate foreign technologies, firms must enhance their in-house R&D capabilities. To respond to these challenges, *the government should consider introducing policy instruments that foster R&D and innovation in the private sector, including direct funding (grants and subsidies), matching grants, and R&D tax credits.*

Facilitating Firm Exit and Restructuring

Georgia ranked 81 out of 183 economies on the 2013 Doing Business indicator on resolving insolvency. Debt recovery takes on average two years, longer than the Organisation for Co-operation and Development (OECD) average of 1.7 years, and costs 4 percent of the bankruptcy estate, compared with the OECD average of 9 percent (figure 5.1). While the cost of recovery is low, the recovery rate in Georgia is 35.7 percent, considerably lower than the OECD average of 70.6 percent (World Bank 2013).

Insolvency in Georgia is limited, particularly when it comes to restructuring. "Insolvency" is legally defined as the inability of a debtor to pay its debts as they become due but does not include a situation in which the sum of a debtor's liabilities exceeds the sum of its assets. The limited definition of insolvency is inconsistent with definitions in other modern insolvency laws.

Restructuring. Restructuring is a critical tool to save a viable yet distressed business. As mentioned above, "insolvency" in Georgia is defined as the inability of the debtor to pay its debts as they become due. It is therefore possible that a viable business with cash flow problems may be forced into insolvency.

Figure 5.1 Insolvency Indicators, 2013

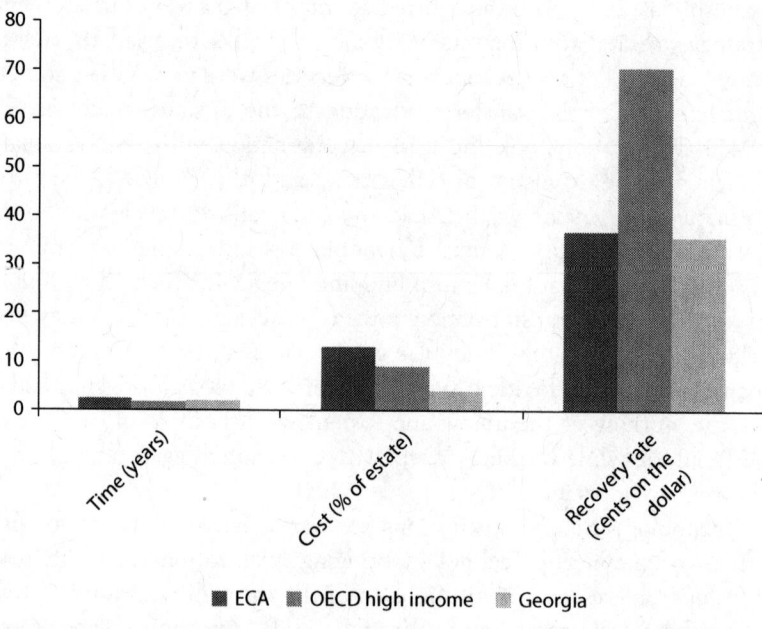

■ ECA ▨ OECD high income ▨ Georgia

Source: World Bank 2013.
Note: ECA = Europe and Central Asia; OECD = Organisation for Economic Co-operation and Development.

To rehabilitate a business that is insolvent but remains viable, additional loans may be required. At present, no mechanism incentivizes such post-petition financing. The unavailability of post-petition financing is a limitation in the framework for reorganization for viable businesses. *The insolvency law should be changed to include incentives that motivate the banking sector to provide post-petition financing.*

Access. For an insolvency regime to be effective, it must be accessible to all stakeholders. In Georgia a debtor may initiate insolvency proceedings upon actual, pending, or potential insolvency. This permits the debtor to be proactive at an early stage of its financial difficulties, potentially increasing the chances of saving a distressed yet viable business. However, it is difficult for a creditor to initiate insolvency proceedings. A creditor seeking to force a debtor into bankruptcy must either show two valid court decisions against the debtor for nonpayment of dues or hold a substantial percentage of the insolvent debtor's debt. This dampens the confidence that creditors have in loan recovery, making them more risk-averse to lend. *Creditors should be allowed to initiate insolvency proceedings to increase their confidence in loan recovery, thus making them less risk-averse to lending.*

Raising Awareness

This chapter has elaborated on how government can facilitate high-growth entrepreneurial activity. In addition to instruments, the government must encourage entrepreneurship in the country. It has a key role to play in raising awareness of the private benefits of undertaking entrepreneurial activities. An example of this was the efforts of the Thatcher government, which came into power in the United Kingdom in 1979 with the clear objective to create an "enterprise culture" (Burrows 1991). The idea was to change the social attitudes of the U.K. population away from what the government perceived as a "dependency culture," in which workers relied on large organizations and the state for employment, to a culture in which individuals strived to start their own businesses and created jobs in the context of an "enterprise culture." *At the basic education level, school curriculum needs to factor in prerequisites that encourage innovative thinking.* An example of a U.K.-based program designed to influence the attitudes of young people toward self-employment is the Shell Technology Enterprise Program, which raises awareness among college students of the benefits of working in a small business through facilitating short-term placements during their summer vacation. Another example of a program aimed at the youth is the Law 44 in southern Italy, which provides a range of financial and advisory support services to individuals ages 18–30 who wishing to start new businesses in that region. *Further, showcasing successful entrepreneurs can go a long way in fostering the entrepreneurship culture in society.* The objective of all the policy instruments reviewed here is to create an entrepreneurship culture and increase the supply of new entrepreneurs as well as ensure their survival and, most important, their growth.

Summary of Policy Recommendations and Timelines

Policy measure	Timeline
Improving efficiency in business environment	
Announce any changes to the tax code at least six months before their implementation to make it easier for firms to follow them.	0–3 months
Increased access to finance	
Establish favorable financing programs for SMEs by developing early-stage risk capital.	6–12 months
Increased access to markets	
Introduce instruments of financial assistance to defray a portion of the cost that firms incur to acquire the requisite capacity to complete on the global market (for example, matching grants to buy business development services).	6–12 months
Provide basic infrastructure to enable firms to adhere to international standards by building accredited control laboratories.	Greater than 1 year
Formulate policies to promote backward links between foreign firms and the domestic economy.	3–6 months
Developing skills	
Reorient higher education programs to produce more industry-relevant skills.	Greater than 1 year
Emphasize industry-relevant vocational training and education courses that cater to the technical needs of the various priority sectors identified by the government.	6–12 months
Increasing firm level R&D and industry-research linkages	
Introduce programs and policies that encourage R&D in firms (for example, R&D tax credits and matching grants).	3–6 months

table continues next page

Fostering Entrepreneurship in Georgia • http://dx.doi.org/10.1596/978-1-4648-0062-7

Summary of Policy Recommendations and Timelines *(continued)*

Policy measure	Timeline
Introduce programs and policies that incentivize industry and researchers to effectively collaborate.	3–6 months
Facilitating firm exit and restructuring	
Change the insolvency law to include incentives that motivate the banking sector to provide post-petition financing.	6–12 months
Allow creditors to initiate insolvency proceedings.	6–12 months
Raising awareness	
Change the school curricula to encourage innovative thinking.	6–12 months
Increase awareness of entrepreneurship by showcasing successful entrepreneurs.	0–3 months

Notes

1. Brazil emphasizes the creation of private venture capital funds, including venture capital incubators, while Chile fosters the creation of business angel networks by financing their operational costs (Kantis and Federico 2011). After investing large amounts of resources in fostering the creation of private venture capital funds, both countries realized that new initiatives designed to specifically address deficiencies in the provision of seed capital were necessary.

2. Either directly or by supporting private institutions, governments promote the creation of information exchanges that could range from lists of inputs and materials available locally—which might include prices and qualities—to names, locations, and profiles of local suppliers.

3. By exempting exporters from a value added tax, governments encourage the use of local inputs; by treating costs incurred in the creation of links as tax-deductible expenses from corporate income tax, governments promote their creation.

4. Firms from non–Organization for Economic Cooperation and Development (OECD) countries score significantly below firms from OECD countries on a measure of management practices (Bloom and Van Reenen 2010).

References

Bloom, N., and J. Van Reenen. 2010. "Why Do Management Practices Differ across Firms and Countries?" London School of Economics and Political Science, Centre for Economic Performance, London.

Burrows, R., ed. 1991. *Deciphering the Enterprise Culture.* London: Routeledge.

Etzkowitz, H., J. Manoel, C. De Mello, and M. Almeida. 2005. "Towards 'Meta-Innovation' in Brazil: The Evolution of the Incubator and the Emergence of a Triple Helix." *Research Policy* 34 (4): 411–24.

Kantis, H. D., and J. S. Federico. 2011. *Entrepreneurial Ecosystems in Latin America: The Role of Policies.* Liverpool, U.K.: Kaufman Foundation.

KISED (Korea Institute of Startup and Entrepreneurship Development). n.d. "What We Do." www.kised.or.kr/new/english/page3.html.

———. 2011. "Startup Korea Blooming the SME Renaissance." http://www.colombo-plan.org/colombo-plan_sitearchives/resources/reports/ppsd/07072011_22072011/SKBSMER.pdf.

Kuriakose, S., I. Goldberg, and C. Zhang. 2011. *Fostering Technology Absorption in Southern African Enterprises.* Washington, DC: World Bank.

Leamon, A., and J. Lerner. 2012. "Creating a Venture Ecosystem in Brazil: FINEP's INOVAR Project." Harvard Business School, Cambridge, MA. www.abvcap.com.br/Download/Artigos/1507.pdf.

Nolan, A. 2003. "Rationale for Public Policy." In *Entrepreneurship and Local Economic Development: Program and Policy Recommendations.* Paris: Organisation for Economic Co-operation and Development.

OECD (Organisation for Economic Co-operation and Development). 2012. *SME Policy Index: Eastern Partner Countries 2012: Progress in the Implementation of the Small Business Act for Europe.* Paris: OECD.

Rothaermel, F. T. 2002. "Technological Discontinuities and Inter-firm Cooperation: What Determines a Start-up's Attractiveness as Alliance Partner?" *IEEE Transactions on Engineering Management* 49 (4): 388–97.

World Bank. 2011. *Doing Business 2012: Doing Business in a More Transparent World.* Washington, DC: World Bank.

———. 2012. *Concept Note: Georgia Sources of Growth Report.* Washington, DC.

———. 2013. "Doing Business." Washington, DC. www.doingbusiness.org/data/exploreeconomies/georgia#resolving-insolvency.

Yusuf, S., and K. Nabeshima. 2011. *Some Small Countries Do It Better: Rapid Growth and Its Causes in Singapore, Finland and Ireland.* Washington, DC: World Bank.

Latent Entrepreneurship

An empirical study of actual entrepreneurial activities alone may overlook the entrepreneurial potential of an economy.[1] Actual entrepreneurs include only people who have successfully started a business and exclude firms and individuals that are truly facing enormous constraints and are unable to enter the market at all. This bias is known in the literature as the "hippopotamus versus camel" problem, which suggests that studies of enterprises and entrepreneurs that are already present in the market ("camels in the desert") may completely miss the constraints faced by those who cannot enter the market ("hippopotamus in the desert").

More than 10 years ago, a new literature on "latent entrepreneurship" emerged using data from a household survey data that asked members of the labor force whether they would rather be self-employed. Some may argue against this measure of latent entrepreneurship, as it captures the pool of all possible entrepreneurs, including subsistence forms of self-employment. In difficult labor markets, self-employment may serve as an alternative to joblessness and may represent little more than a survival strategy rather than a high-impact, job-creating business venture. Nonetheless, the pool of those who would rather be self-employed may also be thought of as representing the entire pool of possible entrepreneurs. Every successful venture has arguably grown from the initial efforts of self-employed individuals. Those who prefer to be self-employed represent all latent entrepreneurs, in other words, "survival" or subsistence entrepreneurs and "opportunity" entrepreneurs alike, and their success appear to be driven by similar individual-level and policy correlates. In addition, this measure of entrepreneurship is comparable across countries.

The pioneering work in this field covered about 20 countries, including four new European Union member countries and the Russian Federation. The study found large numbers of people who would like to be entrepreneurs but the "entrepreneurial spirit" remained dormant. In the absence of suitable data, the literature has largely remained stagnant since then. However, the inclusion of a number of related questions in the 2010 Life in Transition Survey provides a window of opportunity to revisit this literature. Data from the 2010 survey suggest that the pool of latent entrepreneurs in Europe and Central Asia—those who prefer to be self-employed—is generally quite large. About a quarter of the labor force in the region, on average, would rather be self-employed, comparable to the size of the latent entrepreneurs in Western European comparator countries in the same survey. In addition, the desire to be self-employed does not appear to be driven by necessity alone, based on survey respondents' individual characteristics. First, many of the latent entrepreneurs are already gainfully wage-employed. In addition, many are highly educated professionals who are employed as directors or managers of their companies.

Note

1. Prepared by Erwin R. Tiongson based on ongoing work with Hilal Atasoy and others "Latent Entrepreneurship in the Europe and Central Asia Region," (World Bank, Washington, DC, 2013, http://www.iza.org/conference_files/worldb2013/atasoy_h8790.pdf). The results also appear in a forthcoming ECA regional report on jobs.

Classification of Exports by Product and Technology

Table B.1 Classification of Exports by Product and Technology

Total exports		
Primary	Primary (oil)	
	Primary (nonoil)	
Manufactured	Resource-based 1: Agro-based	Resource-based
	Resource-based 2: Other resource-based	
	Low technology 1: Fashion cluster	Low tech
	Low technology 2: Other low tech	
	Medium technology 1: Automotive	Medium tech
	Medium technology 2: Processing	
	Medium technology 3: Engineering	
	High technology 1: Electrical and electronics	High tech
	High technology 2: Other high tech	
Others	Other transactions	

Source: United Nations Commodity Trade Statistics (Comtrade) database 2011.

Data Sources and Regression Results of New Entrepreneurship Survey

Gallup World Poll Data

The Gallup World Poll Database includes more than 18,000 observations from 19 countries in Europe and Central Asia.[1] The data for Armenia, Azerbaijan, and Georgia are based on 1,000 observations for each country. The core Gallup World Poll questionnaire includes detailed information on demographics (such as gender, age, marital status, and education); income; well-being and job satisfaction; confidence and trust in institutions, family, and strangers; and most important, entrepreneurs. Data on self-employment distinguish between full- and part-time employment and indicate the number of hours worked.

New World Bank Entrepreneurship Survey

The total population of firms was provided by the Department of Statistics of Georgia (GeoStat). The database included a detailed breakdown of activities of 57,631 firms (16,705 of them were unidentified business). Keeping in mind the government's priority sectors and the potential for high-growth entrepreneurship, a sample of 300 firms established between 2002 and 2010 was surveyed from among 11,416 firms from sectors including food, chemicals, machinery and equipment, electronics, information technology, transport, pharmacy, telecom, and hotels and restaurants. The distribution of firms surveyed was based on the weighted proportion of the particular sector's contribution to total turnover in 2011.

Box C.1 Specification of Ordinary Least Squares Regression

Dependent variable
Growth = average sales growth of the firm during the last five years (percent)

Independent variables
Firm characteristics
Number of employees = proxy for firm size
  Firm age = age of the firm (years)

Entrepreneur characteristics
Founders' education = 1: at least one founder of the firm has above technical degree; = 0 otherwise
  Founders' age = average age of the founders
  Industry experience = 1: at least one founder has industry experience before the establishment of the firm; = 0 otherwise

Innovative activity
Innovation = 1: the firm introduced a new or substantially improved product or good during the past three years (excluding simple resale of new products purchased from other enterprises and changes of solely aesthetic nature); = 0 otherwise

Strategy
Low cost = 1: main strategy of the firm was to offer standardized products/services at low cost; = 0 otherwise
  Unique product = 1: main strategy of the firm was to offer unique products and services; = 0 otherwise

Funding
Venture capital = 1: received venture capital for setting up the firm; = 0 otherwise
  Bank = 1: attracted funds from a bank for setting up the firm

Market environment
Competition = 1: there are many business competitors; = 0 otherwise
  Technology risk = degree of technology risk/uncertainty in setting up/operating the firm
  Market risk = degree of market risk/uncertainty in setting up/operating the firm

Other firms' sales growth
Other firms' growth = sales growth of other firms in the same sector

  This factor is included as a control variable for two reasons. First, firm sales would be expected to grow faster in fast-growing sectors. Second, the variable is a useful control for other omitted local factors that affect sales growth such as taxes and regulation. Information on how taxes, regulation, and other transaction costs vary across sectors was unobservable for this analysis. This variable should control for such factors.

Box C.2 Specification of the Probit Regression

Dependent variable

Innovation = 1 if the firm introduced a new or substantially improved product or service during the past three years; = 0 otherwise

Independent variables

Firm characteristics

Number of employees = proxy for firm size

Firm age = age of the firm (years)

R&D intensity = average R&D expenditure to sales ratio

High-tech sector = 1 if the firm's industry belongs to high-technology sector; = 0 otherwise

Entrepreneur characteristics

Founders' education = 1 if at least one founder of a firm has above a technical degree; = 0 otherwise

Founders' age = average age of the founders

Technical engineering = 1 if at least one founder's main area of expertise is technical and engineering knowledge; = 0 otherwise

General management = 1 if at least one founder's main area of expertise is general management; = 0 otherwise

Strategy and market environment

International market = 1 if the firm also sells to the international market; = 0 otherwise

R&D activity = 1 if R&D activity is considered important for creating and sustaining the competitive advantage of the firm; = 0 otherwise

Alliances = 1 if alliances with other firms are considered important for creating and sustaining the competitive advantage of the firm.

Controls include sector dummy variables and the innovation rates of other firms in the same sector (in the same sector, number of innovative firms excluding the firm as a proportion of total firms excluding itself).

Table C.1 Regression Results for Ordinary Least Squares Specification

Estimation method	<Armenia> Ordinary least squares	<Georgia> Ordinary least squares	<Azerbaijan> Ordinary least squares
Dependent variable	Growth	Growth	Growth
Independent variables			
Firm characteristics			
Number of employees	0.201* (0.119)	0.123* (0.074)	–0.009 (0.041)
Firm age	–7.191*** (2.228)	0.46 (0.701)	–6.186*** (1.876)
Entrepreneur characteristics			
Founders' education	31.06 (26.858)	–0.567 (6.311)	24.469 (38.392)
Founders' age	–13.375** (5.463)	0.329 (1.656)	4.435 (5.773)
Industry experience	24.263* (14.434)	7.275** (3.483)	–6.864 (9.193)
Innovative activity			
Innovation	20.878* (11.673)	5.906 (6.225)	31.876** (14.484)
Strategy			
Low cost	48.958*** (17.802)	8.784 (8.123)	22.709 (21.695)
Unique product	26.7* (14.972)	5.062 (8.076)	18.945 (22.21)
Funding			
Venture capital	31.971 (92.201)	22.554* (13.557)	–8.252 (54.03)
Bank	–14.506 (14.217)	–2.982 (3.839)	0.228 (11.412)
Market environment			
Competition	–4.292 (10.757)	0.306 (3.313)	–12.198 (9.623)
Technology risk	5.095 (4.306)	0.703 (1.747)	–5.316 (6.604)
Market risk	–5.856 (4.278)	1.884 (1.65)	0.183 (8.248)
Other firms' sales growth			
Other firms' growth	.894*** (0.166)	.964*** (0.272)	0.877** (0.245)
Constant	1.233 (35.357)	–22.198* (13.504)	13.263 (48.814)
N	291	299	299
R^2	0.2278	0.1032	0.1271

Note: Numbers in parentheses are standard errors. Coefficients on sector dummy variables are not reported.
Significance level: * = 10 percent, ** = 5 percent, *** = 1 percent.

Table C.2 Regression Results for Probit Specification

Estimation method	<Armenia> Probit	<Georgia> Probit	<Azerbaijan> Probit
Dependent variable	Innovation	Innovation	Innovation
Independent variables			
Firm characteristics			
Number of employees	0.001 (0.002)	0.004 (0.004)	0.005*** (0.001)
Firm age	−0.027 (0.034)	−0.047 (0.073)	−0.141*** (0.052)
R&D intensity	0.005 (0.006)	0.075** (0.031)	0.026991 (0.023)
High-tech sector	0.012 (0.166)	−0.611 (0.565)	0.188 (0.433)
Entrepreneur characteristics			
Founders education	−0.245 (0.474)	0.321 (0.334)	−0.336 (0.805)
Founders age	−0.104 (0.081)	−0.198 (0.161)	0.147 (0.172)
Technical engineering	−0.35 (0.328)	0.538 (0.647)	0.292 (0.777)
General management	0.352** (0.172)	0.94* (0.493)	−0.121 (0.258)
Strategy and market environment			
International market	0.363** (0.182)	−0.256 (0.518)	0.379 (0.388)
R&D activity	0.12** (0.057)	−0.174 (0.154)	−0.187 (0.162)
Alliances	−0.073 (0.057)	0.069 (0.151)	0.395* (0.204)
Networking	−0.066 (0.064)	0.313** (0.156)	0.035 (0.153)
Product and market	0.353* (0.206)	0.334 (0.306)	0.599** (0.252)
Funding			
External fund	0.096 (0.207)	0.254 (0.348)	−0.548 (0.394)
Other firms' innovation			
Other firms' innovation	0.023*** (0.009)	0.09*** (0.028)	0.035*** (0.011)
Constant	−0.684 (0.718)	−3.879*** (1.079)	−2.509** (1.173)
N	300	300	299
Log likelihood	−171.716	−50.783	−72.414

Note: Numbers in parentheses are standard errors. Coefficients on sector dummy variables are not reported. R&D = research and development.
Significance level: * = 10 percent, ** = 5 percent, *** = 1 percent.

Note

1. For Europe and Central Asia the database does not include data on Albania, Bosnia and Herzegovina, Kosovo, the former Yugoslav Republic of Macedonia, Montenegro, and Serbia.

Regression Results of Enterprise Survey

Table D.1 Sample Size and Distribution of ECA 2008/09 Surveys

	N (firms)	Manu-facturing	Retail, %	Other services, %	Small (5–19), %	Medium (20–99), %	Large (100+), %
Southern Caucasus countries							
Armenia	374	30	33	37	53	32	15
Azerbaijan	380	32	32	37	45	37	18
Georgia	373	33	29	38	49	37	14
Selected ECA comparator countries							
Belarus	273	38	35	27	35	34	31
Bosnia and Herzegovina	361	35	29	36	39	37	24
Bulgaria	288	33	32	35	48	33	18
Czech Republic	250	44	24	32	32	40	28
Estonia	273	34	30	36	41	30	29
Hungary	291	40	21	39	34	33	33
Kazakhstan	544	34	31	36	27	42	30
Kosovo	270	38	23	39	70	25	5
Kyrgyz Republic	235	40	23	37	42	43	16
Latvia	271	34	33	33	34	33	33
Lithuania	276	37	26	37	38	34	27
Macedonia, FYR	366	35	26	39	38	40	22
Moldova	363	30	37	33	34	42	24
Mongolia	362	36	23	41	40	41	20
Montenegro	116	33	35	32	52	34	14
Poland	455	33	29	37	48	28	24
Romania	541	35	28	36	32	34	34
Russian Federation	1,004	71	11	18	24	37	39
Serbia	388	35	26	39	37	32	31
Slovak Republic	275	33	30	37	35	35	30
Slovenia	276	38	20	42	38	30	31
Tajikistan	360	32	30	38	50	36	14
Turkey	1,152	80	9	12	31	39	30

table continues next page

78

Regression Results of Enterprise Survey

Table D.1 Sample Size and Distribution of ECA 2008/09 Surveys *(continued)*

	N (firms)	Manu-facturing	Retail, %	Other services, %	Small (5–19), %	Medium (20–99), %	Large (100+), %
Ukraine	851	68	14	18	39	35	25
Uzbekistan	366	34	30	37	37	37	26

Source: World Bank Enterprise Surveys Database (2013).
Note: ECA = Europe and Central Asia; R&D = research and development.

Table D.2 List of Variables

Innovation variables (indicator 0/1)

ECAo1	Product innovation
ECAo13	Process innovation
In both	Conducted both product and process innovation
In neither	Conducted either product or process innovation
ECAo3	Spent on R&D
e6	Uses foreign-licensed technology

Performance variables (Y)

perf1	Annual sales growth
perf2	Annual employment growth
perf3	Annual labor productivity growth

Explanatory and control variables

wk1	% of firms offering formal training
wk13	% of unskilled workers* (manufacturing only)
logexp_wkrs	Log of capital-expenditures-to-workers ratio: log((n5a+n5b)/s)
exporter	Indicator if firm has at least 10 percent of annual sales derived from direct exports
ownership	Indicator if firm has at least 10 percent foreign ownership
car1	Firm age
Size dummy variables	1 = small (5–19), 2 = medium (20–99), 3 = large (100+)
Sector dummy variables	Garments, food, chemicals, metals and machinery, other manufacturing, retail, other services

Regression structure

	Probit: errors clustered by sector7 (7 industries)
	Ordinary least squares: svy set command

Source: World Bank Enterprise Surveys Database (2013).
Note: R&D = research and development.

Fostering Entrepreneurship in Georgia • http://dx.doi.org/10.1596/978-1-4648-0062-7

Table D.3 Who Innovates? Product Innovation

	Armenia	Azerbaijan	Georgia	Czech Republic	Poland	Russian Federation	Turkey
Exporter	0.0124	0.203	0.355**	−0.0630***	0.0467	0.176***	0.0785
	(0.102)	(0.232)	(0.152)	(0.0228)	(0.0414)	(0.0272)	(0.0600)
Foreign ownership	−0.00290	0.213*	0.00678	0.262***	0.161	0.165***	0.0976
	(0.0425)	(0.120)	(0.0518)	(0.0657)	(0.106)	(0.0308)	(0.155)
% of unskilled workers (manufacturing firms only)	0.000683	0.000792	0.00156	−0.00865	0.00251	0.00257**	0.000447
	(0.00161)	(0.00298)	(0.00163)	(0.00671)	(0.00427)	(0.00114)	(0.00108)
Offers formal training	0.260***	0.256	0.309***	0.0431	0.166**	0.168***	0.0936
	(0.0601)	(0.182)	(0.0892)	(0.194)	(0.0826)	(0.0448)	(0.0723)
Capital expenditures to sales ratio	−0.00192	−0.00130	0.00691*	−0.00600*	−0.00155	−0.00869	0.00127***
	(0.00392)	(0.00121)	(0.00372)	(0.00335)	(0.00114)	(0.00643)	(0.000474)
Log (capital expenditures to workers ratio)	0.0472**	0.0272	0.121***	−0.0918***	−0.0137	−0.0560**	0.0281
	(0.0226)	(0.0347)	(0.0161)	(0.0236)	(0.0181)	(0.0230)	−0.0202

Source: World Bank Enterprise Surveys Database (2013).
Note: Numbers in parentheses are standard errors. Table shows estimates for β from equation 4.1. Probit regression where explanatory variables are regressed individually with control variables. Dependent variable: dummy variable if firm conducted product innovation. Marginal effects are shown. Each regression also controls for age, sector, and firm size group. Excluded dummy variables: other manufacturing and small-size firm. Significance level: * = 10 percent, ** = 5 percent, *** = 1 percent.

Table D.4 Who Innovates? Process Innovation

	Armenia	Azerbaijan	Georgia	Czech Republic	Poland	Russian Federation	Turkey
Exporter	−0.00895	−0.118	0.193***	−0.125	0.156**	0.124***	0.190***
	(0.0985)	(0.271)	(0.0207)	(0.120)	(0.0612)	(0.0204)	(0.0587)
Foreign ownership	0.0166	0.141***	−0.268	0.0124	0.213**	−0.0484	0.126
	(0.0477)	(0.0519)	(0.191)	(0.0367)	(0.0885)	(0.0343)	(0.0974)
% of unskilled workers (manufacturing firms only)	0.000376	0.00435***	0.00427***	−0.00274**	0.00619**	0.00286***	0.00118
	(0.000687)	(0.00147)	(0.000786)	(0.00111)	(0.00295)	(0.000908)	(0.00104)
Offers formal training	0.0141	0.216**	−0.0647	0.0790	0.245***	0.106***	0.180***
	(0.0569)	(0.0949)	(0.0429)	(0.117)	(0.0891)	(0.0249)	(0.0421)
Capital expenditures to sales ratio	−0.00374	0.000236	0.000353	−0.00875***	−0.00206	−0.00585*	0.000645*
	(0.00384)	(0.00124)	(0.000261)	(0.00222)	(0.00270)	(0.00348)	(0.000348)
Log (capital expenditures to workers ratio)	0.0442**	0.00489	−0.0199**	−0.0806***	0.0628**	−0.0361***	0.0248
	(0.0191)	(0.0348)	(0.00988)	(0.0171)	(0.0297)	(0.0123)	(0.0178)

Source: World Bank Enterprise Surveys Database (2013).
Note: Numbers in parentheses are standard errors. Table shows estimates for β from equation 4.1. Probit regression where explanatory variables are regressed individually with control variables. Dependent variable: dummy variable if firm conducted process innovation. Marginal effects are shown. Each regression also controls for age, sector, and firm size group. Excluded dummy variables: other manufacturing and small-size firm. Significance level: * = 10 percent, ** = 5 percent, *** = 1 percent.

Table D.5 Who Innovates? R&D

	Armenia	Azerbaijan	Georgia	Czech Republic	Poland	Russian Federation	Turkey
Exporter	−0.0881*	−0.0231	0.0316	−0.0386	0.250***	0.568***	0.146**
	(0.0524)	(0.0171)	(0.0561)	(0.0410)	(0.0572)	(0.0472)	(0.0603)
Foreign ownership	0.0322	0.00835	−0.0429	−0.0945	0.157**	−0.0688***	−0.00679
	(0.0577)	(0.0173)	(0.0479)	(0.0632)	(0.0713)	(0.0239)	(0.104)
% of unskilled workers (manufacturing firms only)	0.00162	1.44e−08	0.000609	−0.00231*	0.00180	−0.00101**	0.000167
	(0.00120)	(6.25e−08)	(0.000483)	(0.00118)	(0.00250)	(0.000497)	(0.000852)
Offers formal training	−0.00268	9.18e−07	0.621***	0.0642	0.141*	0.322***	0.157***
	(0.236)	(3.85e−06)	(0.0705)	(0.138)	(0.0733)	(0.0382)	(0.0510)
Capital expenditures to sales ratio	0.00156	−0.00152***	−0.00121**	−0.00114	0.00153*	−0.0100***	−0.000423**
	(0.00161)	(0.000127)	(0.000523)	(0.00170)	(0.000823)	(0.00205)	(0.000205)
Log (capital expenditures to workers ratio)	0.0310	0.00667	0.0815	0.00414	0.0101	−0.0285**	−0.00749
	(0.0301)	(0.00959)	(0.0519)	(0.0201)	(0.0228)	(0.0123)	(0.0181)

Source: World Bank Enterprise Surveys Database (2013).
Note: Numbers in parentheses are standard errors. Table shows estimates for β from equation 4.1. Probit regression where explanatory variables are regressed individually with control variables. Dependent variable: dummy variable if firm conducted process innovation. Marginal effects are shown. Each regression also controls for age, sector, and firm size group. Excluded dummy variables: other manufacturing and small-size firm. R&D = research and development.
Significance level: * = 10 percent, ** = 5 percent, *** = 1 percent.

Table D.6 Who Innovates? Foreign-Licensed Technology

	Armenia	Azerbaijan	Georgia	Czech Republic	Poland	Russian Federation	Turkey
Exporter	−0.109	0.108	0.0111	0.0616	0.0109	0.0557	−0.00587
	(0.262)	(0.221)	(0.0926)	(0.0404)	(0.0492)	(0.170)	(0.0499)
Foreign ownership	0.0157	0.190	0.410**	0.233	−0.000761	0.162	0.0721
	(0.0471)	(0.163)	(0.167)	(0.148)	(0.0553)	(0.213)	(0.116)
% of unskilled workers (manufacturing firms only)	0.000291	−0.000854	0.00143	−0.000466	−0.000245	−0.000775	0.000183
	(0.00204)	(0.00248)	(0.00101)	(0.00112)	(0.000647)	(0.000703)	(0.000224)
Offers formal training	0.268	0.636***	0.137**	0.112***	0.0510*	−0.109	0.0799*
	(0.211)	(0.107)	(0.0587)	(0.0252)	(0.0305)	(0.0708)	(0.0434)
Capital expenditures to sales ratio	0.00688**	0.00475***		−0.00289	−0.00226	0.00638	−0.000387
	(0.00277)	(0.00143)		(0.00361)	(0.00365)	(0.00389)	(0.000945)
Log (capital expenditures to workers ratio)	0.0472	0.0937***	0.00107	−0.0149	0.0768**	0.0332	0.0176
Exporter	(0.101)	(0.0232)	(0.00181)	(0.0259)	(0.0302)	(0.0314)	(0.0218)

Source: World Bank Enterprise Surveys Database (2013).
Note: Numbers in parentheses are standard errors. Table shows estimates for β from equation 4.1. Probit regression where explanatory variables are regressed individually with control variables. Dependent variable: dummy variable if firm uses technology that is foreign licensed. Marginal effects are shown. Each regression also controls for age, sector, and firm size group. Excluded dummy variables: other manufacturing and small-size firm.
Significance level: * = 10 percent, ** = 5 percent, *** = 1 percent.

Table D.7 Who Innovates? Pooled Regressions

	Product innovation	Process innovation	Innovated in both	Innovated in either product or process	Spent on R&D	Uses foreign-licensed technology
Exporter	0.213***	0.0712	−0.182***	−0.0910	0.00141	0.0170
	(0.0609)	(0.0841)	(0.0562)	(0.0644)	(0.0242)	(0.127)
Foreign ownership	0.0438	−0.0717	−0.00277	0.0346	−0.00477	0.222**
	(0.0319)	(0.0929)	(0.0302)	(0.0806)	(0.0418)	(0.107)
% of unskilled workers (manufacturing firms only)	0.00125	0.00284***	−0.00113	−0.00270***	0.000578**	0.000465
	(0.00147)	(0.000882)	(0.00135)	(0.000958)	(0.000257)	(0.00133)
Offers formal training	0.311***	0.0132	−0.306***	−0.00687	0.255	0.178***
	(0.0418)	(0.0570)	(0.0401)	(0.0545)	(0.166)	(0.0686)
Capital expenditures to sales ratio	−0.000502	−0.000119	0.000539	9.91e−05	0.000104	0.00574***
	(0.00112)	(0.000426)	(0.00106)	(0.000334)	(0.00118)	(0.00109)
Log (capital expenditures–to–workers ratio)	0.0902***	−0.000716	−0.0894***	0.00179	0.0567*	0.130***
	(0.0207)	(0.0116)	(0.0256)	(0.0113)	(0.0299)	(0.0312)

Source: World Bank Enterprise Surveys Database (2013).
Note: Numbers in parentheses are standard errors. Table shows estimates for β from equation 4.2. Sample includes Armenia, Azerbaijan, and Georgia. Probit regression where explanatory variables are regressed individually with control variables. Dependent variable: dummy variable if firm uses technology that is foreign-licensed. Marginal effects are shown. Each regression also controls for age, sector, and firm size group. Excluded dummy variables: Armenia, other manufacturing, and small-size firm. R&D = research and development. Significance level: * = 10 percent, ** = 5 percent, *** = 1 percent.

Table D.8 Annual Employment Growth and Innovation

	Armenia		Azerbaijan		Georgia	
Product innovation	6.796***	6.580***	3.450**	3.523**	9.091***	9.146***
	(1.904)	(1.913)	(1.477)	(1.498)	(2.327)	(2.294)
Exporter		0.761		−8.53e−05		0.225
		(5.000)		(2.465)		(3.378)
Foreign ownership		−3.752		−1.122		−5.448
		(2.766)		(2.317)		(3.672)
Age (years)	−0.349***	−0.342***	−0.0390	−0.0440	−0.594***	−0.620***
	(0.107)	(0.113)	(0.0412)	(0.0419)	(0.195)	(0.198)
Medium-size	1.826	1.878	0.372	0.501	6.574**	6.451**
	(2.284)	(2.326)	(1.722)	(1.726)	(2.637)	(2.598)
Large-size	0.623	0.746	−0.281	0.125	0.475	1.586
	(2.839)	(3.085)	(1.686)	(1.755)	(3.288)	(3.470)
Garments	3.049	3.635	−3.872	−3.836	2.987	2.875
	(4.981)	(4.992)	(2.542)	(2.550)	(3.634)	(3.628)
Food	9.950	9.812	10.64*	10.50*	−2.864	−4.280
	(7.366)	(7.283)	(5.836)	(5.380)	(4.295)	(5.037)
Chemicals	4.928	4.965	6.114	6.084	3.082	3.883
	(4.465)	(4.664)	(5.352)	(5.305)	(5.665)	(5.586)
Metals and machinery	−0.897	−0.975	0.476	0.154	−1.493	−1.259
	(4.561)	(4.737)	(3.092)	(3.196)	(5.358)	(5.358)

table continues next page

Table D.8 **Annual Employment Growth and Innovation** (continued)

	Armenia		Azerbaijan		Georgia	
Retail	0.582	1.081	−1.449	−1.628	3.865	3.851
	(3.406)	(3.480)	(2.356)	(2.436)	(3.201)	(3.186)
Other services	3.770	4.075	−3.559	−3.696*	9.153**	9.727**
	(3.483)	(3.681)	(2.161)	(2.231)	(3.683)	(3.766)
Constant	10.89***	10.83***	10.70***	10.89***	8.765***	9.102***
	(3.577)	(3.689)	(1.975)	(2.072)	(3.363)	(3.396)
Observations	224	224	250	250	261	261
R^2	0.135	0.142	0.117	0.118	0.332	0.343

Note: Numbers in parentheses are standard errors. Table shows estimates for γ from equation 4.3. Dependent variable is annual employment growth in percentage points. Excluded dummy variables: Armenia, other manufacturing, and small-size firm. Significance level: * = 10 percent, ** = 5 percent, *** = 1 percent.

Table D.9 **Annual Real Sales Growth and Innovation in Georgia**

	Product innovation		Process innovation		R&D	
Innovation activity	9.870**	11.85***	10.87*	11.36**	10.18**	9.486**
	(3.856)	(3.594)	(5.496)	(5.486)	(3.999)	(4.042)
Exporter		−13.74**		−9.718		−6.105
		(6.700)		(6.294)		(5.945)
Foreign ownership		−8.167		−5.772		−7.383
		(7.144)		(6.415)		(7.015)
Age (years)	−1.924***	−2.029***	−1.855***	−1.928***	−2.002***	−2.062***
	(0.348)	(0.339)	(0.385)	(0.381)	(0.346)	(0.346)
Medium-sized	−5.352	−5.025	−4.658	−4.330	−5.455	−5.068
	(4.653)	(4.283)	(5.741)	(5.669)	(5.359)	(5.369)
Large-sized	−0.336	5.744	−0.0235	4.394	−0.874	3.233
	(7.311)	(5.825)	(6.522)	(5.515)	(6.367)	(6.062)
Garments	−0.435	1.744	1.164	2.526	−1.360	−0.772
	(4.056)	(3.883)	(5.300)	(5.549)	(3.841)	(3.616)
Food	−9.017	−3.340	−4.061	0.601	−0.639	0.655
	(7.311)	(7.741)	(6.281)	(7.670)	(6.362)	(7.435)
Chemicals	19.10**	23.11***	19.58**	23.35***	20.94***	22.24***
	(8.134)	(6.683)	(8.254)	(7.607)	(6.805)	(6.496)
Metals and machinery	21.37***	19.44**	24.65***	23.79**	28.23***	27.22***
	(7.641)	(7.526)	(9.183)	(9.166)	(8.647)	(8.722)
Retail	14.12**	13.29**	16.25***	15.72***	15.51***	14.86***
	(5.836)	(5.913)	(5.334)	(5.204)	(5.294)	(5.171)
Other services	20.42***	19.05***	21.90***	20.99***	21.05***	20.21***
	(3.559)	(3.385)	(4.347)	(4.216)	(4.212)	(4.056)
Constant	34.36***	35.61***	27.26***	28.28***	37.33***	38.75***
	(4.590)	(4.418)	(7.074)	(7.017)	(4.348)	(4.229)
Observations	139	139	134	134	141	141
R^2	0.410	0.449	0.384	0.404	0.388	0.403

Source: World Bank Enterprise Surveys Database (2013).
Note: Numbers in parentheses are standard errors. Table shows estimates for γ from equation 4.3. Dependent variable is annual real sales growth in percentage points. Excluded dummy variables: Armenia, other manufacturing, and small-size firm. R&D = research and development. Significance level: * = 10 percent, ** = 5 percent, *** = 1 percent

Reference

World Bank. 2013. Enterprise Surveys database. World Bank: Washington, DC. www
.enterprisesurveys.org.

Environmental Benefits Statement

The World Bank is committed to reducing its environmental footprint. In support of this commitment, the Office of the Publisher leverages electronic publishing options and print-on-demand technology, which is located in regional hubs worldwide. Together, these initiatives enable print runs to be lowered and shipping distances decreased, resulting in reduced paper consumption, chemical use, greenhouse gas emissions, and waste.

The Office of the Publisher follows the recommended standards for paper use set by the Green Press Initiative. Whenever possible, books are printed on 50% to 100% postconsumer recycled paper, and at least 50% of the fiber in our book paper is either unbleached or bleached using Totally Chlorine Free (TCF), Processed Chlorine Free (PCF), or Enhanced Elemental Chlorine Free (EECF) processes.

More information about the Bank's environmental philosophy can be found at http://crinfo.worldbank.org/crinfo/environmental_responsibility/index.html.